BOOKBINDING MADE EASY

A Colonial Bookbinder

BOOKBINDING
made easy

LEE M. KLINEFELTER

COLLEGE OF WILLIAM AND MARY
NORFOLK, VIRGINIA

REVISED EDITION

THE BRUCE PUBLISHING COMPANY
MILWAUKEE

Library of Congress Catalog Card Number: 60–11592

© 1960 THE BRUCE PUBLISHING COMPANY

Made in the United States of America

Introduction

IF CHRISTOPHER COLUMBUS were to return to earth today, one of the things in daily use that he would easily recognize would be a book. While man's food, clothing, housing, and transportation have gone through innumerable changes in the past 500 years, the book of today is still very much like the book of the fifteenth century. It is made in much the same way and from very similar materials. Yet in spite of our daily use of books and the fact that bookbinding is one of the world's major industries, the average person knows less about the actual process than he does about the making of an automobile or a suit of clothing. The reason for this seems difficult to understand, but is probably due to the fact that books in their present form have been a familiar part of our daily life from our earliest remembrance. Like our daily bread, we take them for granted and give little thought to how they are made.

Though bookbinding is now almost entirely a machine process, the steps in the process are essentially the same as those used by the hand binder, and the craftsmanship of the hand binder is still widely appreciated. The individuality, beauty, and long-lasting utility of hand-bound books insure a place of honor in any library. While the amateur cannot expect to equal immediately the craftsmanship of the professional binder, he can, by careful attention to the procedure outlined here, make valuable and attractive books from magazines or other printed material and add many years of useful life to volumes that have succumbed to the ravages of use and time.

Much may be said for bookbinding as a school activity. It teaches a respect for books while it provides a means for making and remaking them. It correlates well with the study of literature, history, science, and the languages. Probably its wider practice in schools has been hindered by the nature of the manuals on the subject. Almost without exception, these attempt to cover the entire art, with all its complexities and ramifications, and leave the student with a confused awe for the difficulty of the craft. Since these books, as a rule, have been written by professional binders, they generally call for complete professional equipment, which is out of the question for the average individual.

In the pages that follow, no attempt will be made to duplicate the many texts on the subject, nor to follow religiously the professional methods of binding. The only aim will be to present, in a simple and orderly way, a method of binding suitable for rebinding old books, or preserving magazines and other printed material. The use of easily obtained materials and simple equipment that can be made at home or in the school shop will be suggested so that the difficulty of obtaining special materials and equipment will be obviated.

The difficult art of gold-leaf stamping is discussed, but is recommended only to those who have mastered the art of binding and are, like Alexander, looking for other worlds to conquer.

The student, as he gains skill and familiarity with the craft, will discover short cuts and desirable variations in the steps given here. The study of other books on the subject is, of course, desirable and will reveal many further possibilities. Visits to a local bindery, or the assistance and instruction of a practical binder, will add to the interest of the work and at the same time simplify the more difficult steps.

Contents

CONTENTS

BOOKBINDING MADE EASY

Chapter 1 / Bookbinding: Its Beginnings

WHILE we tend to associate bookbinding with printing, the art of binding was far advanced before the appearance of the first books printed from movable type. There is evidence that as early as the fifth century, Greek scrolls and parchments were cut into sheets and bound between covers. During the centuries that passed before the invention of printing as we now know it, hand-lettered and engrossed manuscripts were bound into books for convenient use and to ensure their preservation. In the early 1400's, the xylographic or block book appeared, printed from engraved wooden blocks. Thus, during the thousand years before 1455 the process of binding was being developed, until in that year or early in 1456, the Gutenberg Bible was published. This book has been generally accepted as the first of

Fig. 1.
An Eleventh Century
Binding.

Fig. 2.
A Fifteenth Century
Reading Desk.

the flood of books that has covered the civilized world since the invention of movable type. By that time binding had reached a state of perfection that has seldom been surpassed. It can well be said that the book appeared then as a finished product, and the centuries since have done little to improve it.

The first books were sewed on leather thongs or bands of parchment, the ends of which were laced into wooden side boards. The back was usually covered with leather and the boards of important or valuable books were frequently decorated with inlays of gold, silver, ivory, enamel, and precious stones. Figure 1 shows such a binding used to cover an eleventh-century Evangelarium, or Book of the Gospels.

By Gutenberg's time, leather was generally used to cover both the boards and back of books, the cords forming ridges across the back. In the course of time the use of wooden boards was discontinued because of their weight and bulk, as well as their susceptibility to damage or destruction by insects, worms, and rot. Pasteboard, made by pasting together sheets of scrap or wastepaper, replaced wooden boards until comparatively modern times. An interesting sidelight on this practice is the fact that a number of rare and valuable printings have been recovered by soaking apart the boards of old bindings.

The practice of decorating the leather covers of books with designs stamped or pressed into the leather was common during the fifteenth century, to be followed in the later years of this century by the use of gold-leaf decoration. The first bound books were intended to lie flat on shelves or slanted reading stands, so they often had brass bosses on the corners of the boards to prevent damage to the binding in sliding over the shelves. In Figure 2, a woodcut reproduced from the "Ship of Fools," a fifteenth-century satire by Sebastian Brandt, we see a typical reading desk of the day. It is interesting to note that even at that early date, there were those who doubted the need for so many books, for the clown is quoted as saying, "I have first place among fools, I possess heaps of volumes that I rarely open. If I read them, I forget them, and am no wiser."

As the number of books increased, it became necessary to stand them on bookshelves in order to conserve space. This exposed the undecorated back to view, and led to the sinking of the cords into the back, and provided a smooth surface suitable for decoration. About the middle of the sixteenth century, in the interest of sound binding, the cords were again allowed to stand out, the title and other decoration being stamped between them.

Fig. 3.
A Sixteenth Century
Bookbinder's Shop.

The name of Jean Grolier is often associated with fine bindings. Grolier was not himself a binder, but a French government financial agent, and eventually became Treasurer-General of France from 1545 until his death in 1565. He was a lover of beautiful books and assembled a library of the finest products of French and Italian binders. Many of his books were bound to his order and decorated in designs suggested by him.

The bookbinder's shop of this period is shown in Figure 3, a reproduction of a woodcut appearing in a German book published in 1568, whose title claims it to be "A Description of All Occupations on Earth." The woodcut is by Jost Ammon and the verse by Hans Sachs. One worker in the background is sewing a book on cords, while another in the foreground is cutting or planing a book with the plow. A book is in a press at the left, and tools of the trade are displayed on the wall. The following verse accompanied the original picture: "I bind all kinds of books, both sacred and secular, large and small, in parchment or only boards, and fit them with good clasps and buckles, and I stamp them ornamentally. I also plane them in the beginning. Finally I gild the cut and thus I earn much money."

The twin arts of printing and binding came to America during the early Colonial period. Though Benjamin Franklin is probably the best known of our early printers, the industries were well established here before his time. The first book to be published and bound in the American Colonies, the "Book of Psalms," also known as the Bay Psalm book, was issued in 1640. It was probably bound by John Saunders, a "bookbynder" who established a shop in 1637. John Ratcliffe came to Boston in 1663 to bind the Eliot Indian Bible, and during the next twenty years is known to have made many notable bindings.

Early American bindings were commonly of leather, and being generally used for books of a serious and practical nature, as a rule they were not elaborately decorated. In the early 1800's, although leather was still used for binding dictionaries, schoolbooks, and other volumes likely to see hard wear, cheaper books were bound in paper-covered boards with leather backs. Because the cheaper grades of leather used in such bindings had a tendency to crack and wear poorly, cloth came into use as a substitute. In turn, this led to the full cloth covers so commonly used today.

The principal changes that have taken place in binding in recent years have had to do with mechanization and cost reduction. Edition binding has become a factory process, rather than an art or craft. Books are made to last years instead of centuries. All this is of course a necessity if books are to be made available to our millions at prices they can afford to pay. There are, to be sure, still a few craftsmen capable of binding a book by the old hand methods, but modern wage scales and material costs are such that special bindings are used only occasionally on books where cost is no consideration. This means that more and more hand binding will be done by amateurs, students, and book lovers, whose reward will be their pleasure in mastering an interesting and historic craft; and their satisfaction in having preserved printed material in books that are both decorative and useful.

Chapter 2 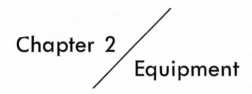 Equipment

THE equipment for bookbinding may be simple or elaborate, costly or inexpensive, as desired. While complete professional equipment may simplify some operations, it is in no way a necessity. The equipment described here will make possible a workmanlike job, and can be made at very little cost by anyone handy with tools.

The first piece of equipment to be used is the sawing clamp shown in Figure 4. It consists of two pieces of soft wood of about the dimensions given, held together by bolts and wing nuts.

Next comes the sewing frame shown in Figure 5. This is best made from soft wood which will take thumbtacks easily. The dimen-

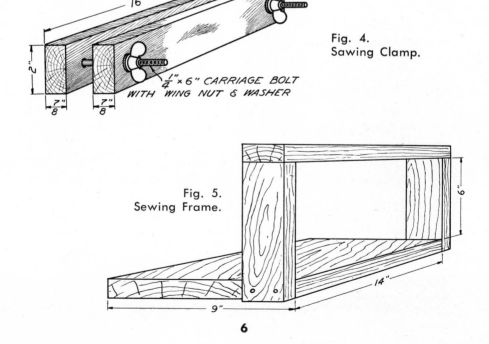

Fig. 4.
Sawing Clamp.

$\frac{1}{4}$" × 6" CARRIAGE BOLT
WITH WING NUT & WASHER

Fig. 5.
Sewing Frame.

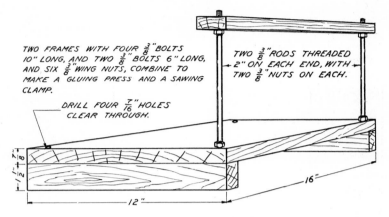

TWO FRAMES WITH FOUR ⅜"BOLTS
10" LONG, AND TWO ⅜"BOLTS 6" LONG,
AND SIX ⅜"WING NUTS, COMBINE TO
MAKE A GLUING PRESS AND A SAWING
CLAMP.

DRILL FOUR 7/16"HOLES
CLEAR THROUGH.

TWO ⅜"RODS THREADED
2" ON EACH END, WITH
TWO ⅜"NUTS ON EACH.

7/8"
1½"
12"
16"

Fig. 6. Burgess Sewing Frame.

sions of the drawing need not be followed closely, but the opening
of the frame should be 3 or 4 inches wider than the length of the
largest book to be sewed.

A sewing frame following more closely the commercial type of
frame is one developed for club use by Mr. J. W. Burgess at the
Ruffner Junior High School, Norfolk, Va., and shown in Figure 6.
In this frame the standards are two threaded steel rods with nuts
screwed on both ends. The ends of the rods slip into holes drilled
through the base and crossbar. The frame can be quickly taken apart
for storage. A feature of it is that the two bases with four bolts and
wing nuts make a gluing press, while the two crossbars with two
bolts and nuts make a sawing clamp.

The gluing and backing press serves several purposes, and requires
more care in building (Fig. 7). It should be made from hardwood,
smoothly planed, or from heavy plywood. The strips of steel screwed
to the beveled edges should be filed flush on the inside face, and the
strips screwed on the square edges will overhang about 3/32 of an inch
on the inside, as shown in Figure 7. Four bolts and washers with wing
nuts complete the press.

If considerable work is to be done, several gluing presses will be
needed, unless they are supplemented by a "nipping" or "standing"
press. An abandoned letter press may be used, or a press can be
built in the shop. Unless a screw-cutting lathe is available, a common bench screw can be bought at little cost to build into a press.

With a standing press, gluing boards should be slipped between

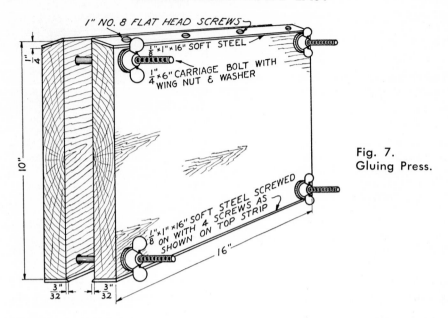

Fig. 7.
Gluing Press.

the books when several are in the press at the same time. These boards should be about ½ inch larger than the books and from ¼ to ½ inch thick. Built-up panels of plywood are satisfactory since they lie flat and do not warp easily.

Pressing tins will be needed and should be about the size of the pressing boards. They are used when gluing on and covering the boards, and prevent moisture from glue or paste working into the book. They also prevent the covered boards from sticking to the fly-leaves if excess glue or paste should squeeze out; when used on the outside of a book they insure a smooth cover even though the press or gluing boards may not be perfectly smooth.

Cutting is one of the most important steps in binding and one

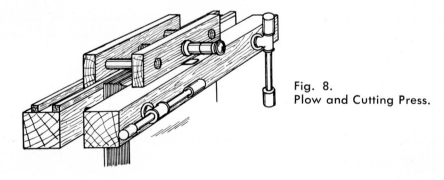

Fig. 8.
Plow and Cutting Press.

requiring much care if it is to be properly done. For many years, in fact almost from the beginning of bookbinding as we know it, the plow and cutting press were the accepted equipment for cutting books. The printers' paper cutter, if available, is faster and somewhat simpler to operate, but every binder should learn to use the plow, and the amateur may well use it in preference to other means.

As shown in Figures 8 and 9, the plow and press are not difficult to make. An old plane iron sharpened as shown in the drawing serves as a cutter. Two bench screws will be needed for the press. When turned bottom up it becomes a "lying press," with a number of uses. It may be used for backing, if backing boards (Fig. 10) are made. It is also useful when stamping.

For cutting millboard, a card cutter is a convenience but by no means a necessity. A pair of heavy shears or tinners' snips can be used. For perfectly straight edges, a sharp knife and steel square

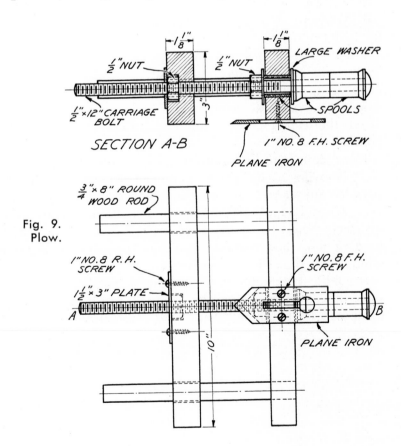

Fig. 9.
Plow.

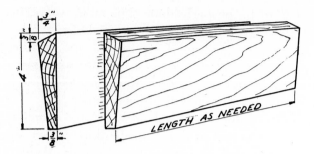

Fig. 10.
Backing Boards.

should be used, or the boards may be clamped up in the cutting press and cut with the plow.

The hammer for rounding and backing should have a broad, rounding face. An ordinary shoemakers' hammer will do nicely for the amateur, especially if shaped up a little with a smooth file.

Paste brushes, a sharp knife, a few discarded razor blades, and a pair of shears will be needed. Special needles for book sewing can be had from dealers, but darning needles will serve as well.

Folders are useful for rubbing down pasted surfaces, creasing backs, and cutting pages. Inexpensive bone and plastic folders can be bought, or wooden ones can be made from maple or other hard wood. They should be about 1¼ by 8 inches, and ³⁄₁₆ inch thick along the center, have rounded edges, and be well waxed and polished.

Paste cloths will be found useful for rubbing down pasted surfaces and removing excess paste or glue. Cheesecloth cut to convenient sizes, or any clean absorbent rags, will do.

A plentiful supply of paste papers, made by cutting newspapers in quarters, should be on hand. Cleanliness being an essential of a neat binding job, these papers should be used freely when pasting or gluing, and discarded as used.

If gold-leaf stamping is to be done, a type holder, type, pallet, and some other equipment will be needed. Details concerning this equipment will be found in Chapter 10 on Finishing.

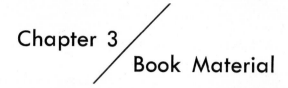

Chapter 3
Book Material

BOOKS are made up of a number of sections, sometimes called "signatures," each section consisting of from 4 to 64 pages. With few exceptions, the pages of each section are printed together on one large sheet, so arranged that when the sheet is folded in a certain way the pages will be in their proper order.

Paper was formerly made to certain sizes as follows. Some of these papers were also available in sheets double the size given.

Writing Papers

Pott	12½ x 15
Foolscap	13½ x 16½
Double foolscap . .	16½ x 26½
Foolscap and third .	13¼ x 22
Foolscap and half .	13¼ x 24¾
Pinched post . . .	14½ x 18½
Small post	15¼ x 19
Large post	16½ x 21
Medium	18 x 23
Standard	17 x 22

Drawing and Book Papers

Demy	15½ x 20
Medium	17¾ x 22½
Royal	19 x 24

Super-royal . . .	19¼ x 27
Imperial	22 x 30
Elephant	23 x 28
Double elephant . .	26½ x 40
Colombier . . .	23½ x 34½
Atlas	26 x 34
Antiquarian . . .	31 x 53
Standard	24 x 36

Printing Papers

Demy	17½ x 22½
Double foolscap . .	17 x 27
Royal	20 x 25
Double crown . . .	20 x 30
Imperial	22 x 30
Standard	25 x 38

These sizes are not used for books at the present time, since books usually are printed in editions large enough to justify the making of paper in any size suitable to the page size wanted.

Modern book papers are designated by their finish, such as Machine Finish, English Finish, Supercalendered, Enameled, and Antique, and are made in the following sizes. These papers up to and including 32 x 44 also are available in sheets of double the size given.

22 x 32	25 x 40	28 x 42	32 x 44
24 x 36	26 x 29	28 x 44	33 x 46
24 x 38	26 x 40	29 x 45	34 x 44
25 x 38	27 x 34	30½ x 41	35 x 45

The number of leaves or pages from a sheet is indicated by the traditional names as follows:

Folio . . . .   2 leaves or 4 pages
Quarto or 4to . . . .   4 leaves or 8 pages
Octavo or 8vo . . . .   8 leaves or 16 pages
Duodecimo or 12mo . . . . . 12 leaves or 24 pages
Sextodecimo or 16mo . . . . 16 leaves or 32 pages

The combination of paper size and fold indicates the page size. As an example, a Royal octavo book will be made up of sections of 8 leaves folded from a Royal (20 by 25) sheet, giving a page size of 6¼ by 10 inches before trimming.

Since the printing of a book is beyond the scope of most amateur binders, and the purchase of the printed sheets from publishers is not always possible, a fertile field lies in the rebinding of old books or the making of new ones from magazines. In every home there are magazines worth preserving in a permanent form, or books that the wear and tear of time have made unusable. These are the raw materials most readily available for the student binder.

One type of monthly magazine most generally bound is about 7 by 10 inches in size and contains, besides advertising confined to the front and back pages, from 100 to 140 pages of reading matter and pictures made into 10 to 15 sections stapled together, with the cover glued on. Six numbers, beginning with the January or July number, make up a volume, the page numbers running consecutively through the reading matter and pictures (but not the advertising) of the entire volume. A printed index for each volume may be obtained, and should be bound into the front of the book.

Another type of magazine frequently bound, about 9 by 12 inches

Fig. 11.
The Raw Material.

Fig. 12. Pulling Apart One-Section Magazines.

in size, has only one section, sometimes containing sixty or more pages, but oftentimes less (Fig. 12). Six or twelve numbers of this magazine with index make a complete volume.

Whether or not an old book should be rebound depends on so many factors that no general rule can be laid down. If the contents of the book are of sufficient value, it may be bound regardless of its condition. As a general rule, it does not pay to rebind a book if pages are badly torn or missing, or the sections are badly worn at the hinge.

A book which is valued for its age or rarity should not be rebound or repaired without the advice of experts, for much or all of its value may be destroyed in rebinding.

Good books issued in paper covers may be given attractive board covers, while valuable pamphlets or bulletins are more easily preserved when bound separately or in groups in board covers.

Chapter 4
Auxiliary Materials

THE materials needed will vary with the type of book and its binding, and, with the exception of material for gold-leaf stamping, are included in this chapter. Material for gold-leaf work is described in Chapter 10 on Finishing.

End papers should be of good quality and weight. A few sheets in white and colors can be obtained from a local printer or a paper supply house at small cost. Bond, antique, kraft, coated, and many other kinds and finishes are made, so there should be no difficulty in finding suitable paper. For many books, brown wrapping paper will serve.

Several kinds of cover cloth may be had from binders' supply houses. For library binding, buckram and fabrikoid are usually used. Buckram is a strong, coarsely woven cotton cloth that has been a favorite cover material for many years, particularly for large and heavy books. Fabrikoid is a pyroxylin coated cotton cloth often given an imitation leather grain or other ornamental surface pattern. It is strong, washable, and a very practical material for books subjected to hard wear. Bookcloth is a medium weight cotton cloth of the type commonly used for edition binding. Like buckram and fabrikoid, it comes in many attractive colors. Some grades are waterproof and are preferable for amateur binders.

Duck, khaki, or denim will be found to be satisfactory cover materials for books subject to hard wear, such as textbooks or bound volumes of magazines used in the shop.

For low-cost bindings, paper-covered boards are often satisfactory and make attractive jobs. Cover papers come in many colors, textures, weights, and finishes. Any local printer or supply house carries some attractive varieties at low cost. Samples of wallpaper with small all-over designs may be had from wallpaper dealers. Contact wallpaper is used for some books.

Board material made especially for use on books is available at paper supply houses. It is called binder's board, cover board, or mill-board, and comes in various weights or thicknesses. Board material from $\frac{1}{16}$ to $\frac{3}{32}$ inch in thickness will be adequate for most books if a hard variety is used. Ordinary cardboard or tablet backs may be used for small books. If used on larger books, two pieces of cardboard should be glued together to make double boards.

For reinforcing the backs of books a heavily starched, open weave cloth called "super" is commonly used. Its principal advantages are that it is inexpensive and that glue passes through it easily. For heavy books and those subject to much wear, a heavier cloth such as "backing flannel" is recommended. This is a strong, closely woven, unbleached cotton material with a nap on one side. It is sold by binders' supply houses. The nap improves its gluing qualities. Ordinary domestic cotton flannel or any strong cotton cloth may be used.

Factory-bound books are machine sewed, while hand-bound books are sewed on cords or tapes. Though tape is more satisfactory for amateur binding, the use of both tape and cord will be discussed in the following pages.

Binders' cord is a soft hemp, cotton, or linen cord of long fiber stock. It should not be too tightly twisted, because the ends must be frayed out.

Unbleached tape should be used, if possible, but ordinary white twilled cotton tape will do very well. It is available in department stores or the "five and ten cent" stores in various widths. If old books are to be rebound, several widths from $\frac{3}{8}$ to 1 inch should be on hand to fit the spaces of the former sewing. For magazines, $\frac{3}{4}$-inch tape is recommended.

Thread is most important, for upon it depends the strength of the book. If it can be obtained, unbleached linen bookbinders' thread should be used, its size depending upon the number and thickness of the sections. In a book with only a few heavy sections, heavy thread should be used, while a book of many thin sections should be sewed with fine linen or silk thread, so as not to add too much thickness to the back. If linen thread cannot be obtained, strong cotton thread, about No. 10 or 12, may be used for most books. Smaller sizes of cotton or strong silk thread should be used for thinner sections.

Paste is used in considerable quantities and may be bought ready-made, or it can be made up as needed. If a large quantity is required, homemade flour paste will be more economical.

A good flour paste can be made with ½ cup of flour and ½ ounce of powdered alum. This is mixed well, water is added to form a thin paste, and the mixture is stirred until it is smooth and free from lumps. Two cups of water are then added and the mixture is boiled about five minutes and stirred to prevent lumping. Three or four drops of oil of cloves will help to preserve the paste. It will keep a week or more and should be made in quantities which will be used in that time. If the paste is too thick, it may be thinned with warm water.

Commercial pastes have the advantage of being ready-made and of keeping better than the homemade product. Several brands of commercial paste have been found suitable for binding and reasonable in cost if bought in pints or quarts.

Glue for binding may be either the ready-to-use type of glue or hot glue. Liquid glue is convenient and generally satisfactory, but sometimes does not dry well in damp weather, and is more expensive than hot glue. If hot glue is to be used, the best grade of hide glue should be obtained. It should be soaked overnight and cooked in a double cooker or electric cooker. Glue should not be made up in large quantities nor overheated, for repeated heating and over-heating weakens it.

A very satisfactory flexible glue may be purchased ready-made, or can be prepared by the user. The following proportions have been found satisfactory.

> 1 lb. dry hide glue
> ½ lb. glycerin
> 1 pint water
> a pinch of moth flakes

Soak the glue overnight in a mixture of water and glycerin. Heat in a double cooker, adding moth flakes, which prevent molding. Avoid the use of excessive heat and repeated heating.

Padding and tabbing cements sold by printers' supply houses are frequently quite satisfactory substitutes for glue or paste in binding operations. Some of these cements are especially recommended for cementing the backs of sewed books and those made up of single sheets. They are strong, flexible, and not affected by atmospheric or climatic conditions — an advantage over most liquid glues. Being already prepared, cement naturally is more convenient than hot glue, though considerably more expensive.

A small, stiff paste brush for repair work will be needed. For pasting and gluing large surfaces, a larger brush will save time. An inexpensive 1-inch paint brush with the bristles cut to about a 1½-inch length will do very well.

Gluing tins will be found very useful when covering books. They may be of bright tin or, better still, sheet aluminum. In either case, they should be of as light a gauge of metal as you can get. Four pieces, about 7 by 10 inches, and four, 9 by 12 inches, will take care of most of your needs.

Chapter 5

Repairing and Sewing

PULLING AND REPAIRING

THE first step in binding a book is separating the material into sections. Old books can be classified either as those in which the sewing is good, or those in which the sewing is broken or pulled out. Books of the first class generally can be repaired without resewing. Such books should not be pulled apart, but Chapter 8 should be referred to and that procedure followed. For books that must be resewed, the steps are as follows:

1. Pulling apart a book. (a) An old book. With a sharp knife or razor blade, cut along the sides of the back through the super or reinforcing cloth. Also cut the thread between the sections (Fig. 13). Pull out the threads and stack the sections in order. If there is hard glue on the back, soften it with a wet cloth before pulling the book apart. Scrape off all the old glue from the back or hinge of the sections.

Fig. 13.
Pulling Apart an Old Book.

Fig. 14.
Repairing
Damaged
Leaves.

b) **Magazines of several sections.** Strip off the cover and pull out the staples with a screw driver or pliers. Bend the magazine back and forth to break loose the glue on the back. Beginning at the front, carefully remove the sections one by one. Discard any pages of advertising which you do not care to save by cutting them off about ½ inch from the hinge. In some cases, entire sections of advertising can be discarded. Some persons, however, prefer to retain and bind in the advertising pages for their interest and value in future years. Save one of the magazine covers for possible use on the book cover.

c) **Magazines of one section.** Remove the staples and discard any advertising pages which you do not wish to preserve. Save the best cover for possible use on the book cover, or you may include all covers in the binding if they are worth saving.

2. Knocking out grooves. This step is necessary only when re-binding an old book. When taken apart, the outer sections will be found to bend outward at the hinge, due to backing. Knock this bend out before going further. Lay a sheet of clean paper on a smooth metal or hardwood surface. (The professional binder uses a "knock-ing-down iron" clamped in his lying press.) Place a section on the paper and hammer along the groove until it is smoothed out. Use a hammer with a broad face and rounded edges, and be careful not to cut the sections with the edge of the hammer. To prevent marking, cover the section with a sheet of wastepaper while hammering. Proceed as above with all the sections.

3. Repairing damaged sections. Occasionally the outer sheet or

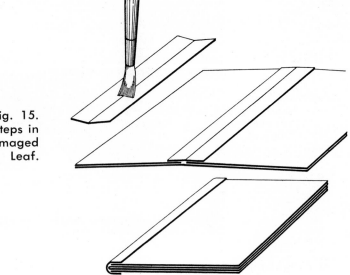

Fig. 15.
Three Steps in
Repairing a Damaged
Leaf.

sheets of some sections will be found entirely or nearly worn through at the hinge. Before going further with the binding process, repair these sections as follows: Cut strips of white paper about 1 inch wide, the length of the pages of the book. Fold these strips down the center, spread paste evenly on them, and fit them over the hinge of the damaged sheets as shown in Figures 14 and 15.

4. Tipping in loose sheets or plates.   Frequently, when rebinding old books, pictures are found to be held in place by a narrow strip of paste along one edge. The operation by which this is done is known as "tipping in." Such pages, if not loosened by wear, become separated when pulling the book apart, and should be tipped in again. To do this, cover all but about ⅛ inch of the hinge edge of the loose

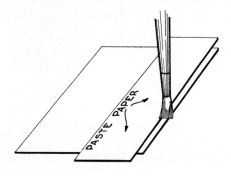

PASTE PAPER

Fig. 16.
Preparing a Sheet for
Tipping In.

page or plate with a paste paper, and spread paste evenly along the exposed edge, as shown in Figure 16. Remove the paste paper and place the page in its proper position in the book.

ASSEMBLING

Carefully assemble and collate the sections. The misplacement, omission, or inversion of sections not discovered at this time will be difficult to rectify.

1. Putting sections in place.   Put together in their proper order the sections that are to make up the book. If you are binding a volume of magazines for which an index is printed, be sure to include it. It is generally placed at the front.

2. Checking or "collating."   Run carefully through the book to see that every page is in its proper place and all sections are right side up.

MAKING END PAPERS

End papers give a finished appearance to a book, protect the first pages of printed matter, and serve as a place for the owner to write his name and any notes or comments he may wish to preserve.

1. Cutting and folding end papers.   Secure four sheets of paper of such size that when folded once the sheet will be about ½ inch larger than the page of the book in both length and width. To illustrate, if the book page is 7 by 10 inches, the paper used should be about 10½ by 15 inches, so as to fold to 7½ by 10½ inches. The paper used for end papers should be similar in weight and quality to that on which the book is printed. Two of the sheets may be colored or

Fig. 17.
Pasting Up
End Papers.

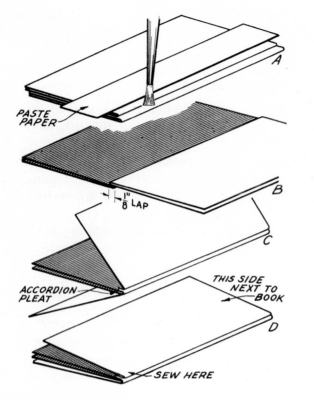

PASTE
PAPER

$\frac{1}{8}$" LAP

A

B

C

ACCORDION
PLEAT

THIS SIDE
NEXT TO
BOOK

D

SEW HERE

Fig. 18.
Making End Papers.

decorated in imitation of the fancy end papers sometimes found in books. Fold these sheets down the center.

When rebinding an old book that is to be put back into the original case, end papers consisting of only a single folded sheet at the front and back usually will be enough. If this is done, fold only two sheets, either white or colored, and omit the following steps 2 and 3.

2. Pasting end papers. After folding the four sheets, stack them in such a way that each exposes about ⅛ inch of the hinge edge of the sheet below it. A paste paper should cover all but the same amount of the top sheet (Fig. 17, and A, Fig. 18). When stacked, spread paste over the exposed edges, and put the sheets together in pairs, one colored and one white sheet making each pair if two colors are used, with the hinge edges lapped as far as the paste has been applied, and the sheets extending in opposite directions as shown at B, Figure 18. Press well and allow to dry.

3. Refolding and placing end papers. When dry, fold one page of the white sheet back over the colored sheet. Then fold the other

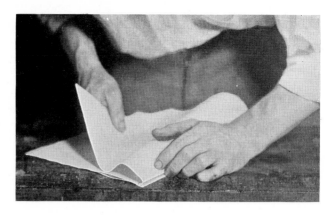

Fig. 19.
Folding
End Papers.

white page back upon itself to make an "accordion pleat" as shown in Figure 19. If more than one white flyleaf is wanted, fold another sheet and insert it in the fold to be sewed. Place the end papers at the front and the back of the book, with the accordion pleat next to the book (C and D, Fig. 18).

SAWING

Sawing is the method used for perforating the back or hinge of the sections to let the needle through when sewing. When books are rebound, it is generally possible to find perforations from the original sewing in such position that tapes can be run between them. In such cases, omit this step.

1. Jogging up and clamping. Jog up the stack of sections so that the head and back are square, and clamp it in the sawing clamp about $\frac{1}{16}$ inch from the back. To jog up a book, hold it loosely in the hands and tap the end or back on the bench several times until the sections are even on the edge being tapped.

2. Marking for tapes or cords. With a pencil and try square draw a line across the back about $\frac{3}{4}$ inch from each end (Fig. 20). Place the end tape about 1 inch inside of these end marks, and the two marks for each tape about $\frac{1}{16}$ inch farther apart than the width of the tape. On large books, space a third or fourth tape evenly between the two end tapes. Square pencil lines across on each of the marks. The book can be marked from the tapes, or the tapes put on the sewing frame to suit marks put on the book.

If cords are to be used, make only one mark for each cord. As a rule, however, more cords are used than tapes. In a book of ordi-

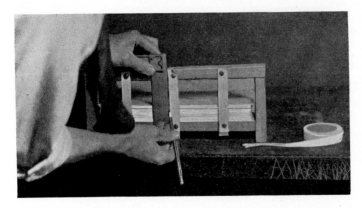

Fig. 20.
Marking Up
From the Tapes.

nary size do not have less than four or five cords, and in larger books have more.

Leave unequal spaces between the end marks and the first tapes or cords, so that there will be no possibility of getting the sections reversed when sewing.

After marking up, remove the end papers or drop them down about ⅛ inch in the frame, so that they will not be cut in sawing. This is done to avoid unsightly saw cuts inside the covers.

3. Sawing. For tapes, cut with a panel or backsaw carefully across the back along each mark (Fig. 21). Saw about ¹⁄₁₆ inch deep which should be enough to cut through the back of each section.

Fig. 21. Sawing.

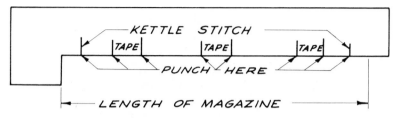

Fig. 22. Marking a Magazine.

For very thick sections, such as single-section magazines, it may be necessary to go deeper.

For cords, cut a groove across the back at each mark large enough for the cord to sink in flush with the back. The end cuts for kettle stitching are the same as for tapes (see step 3 in Sewing).

When thick, single-section magazines are bound, saw cuts deep enough to reach the center pages of the sections will make unsightly gashes in the outer pages. These may be avoided by punching holes instead of sawing them. A convenient method is to make a gauge from a piece of stiff cardboard 3 or 4 inches wide and a few inches longer than the magazines being bound. This is cut and marked as shown in Figure 22. In using it, the magazine is opened to the center, the gauge hooked tightly against the top, and a hole punched through the back or hinge at each mark on the gauge. Use a sharp awl or an ice pick ground to a long sharp point.

SEWING

Modern machine-bound books are sewed together on a special model of sewing machine. Such books are a necessity if thousands of copies are to be produced cheaply, but they are neither as strong nor as lasting as those well bound by hand on tapes or cords.

In a style of binding formerly much used, the cords were raised instead of being sawed into the back as directed under Sawing. The leather covering was glued directly to the back of the sections and pinched up around the cords. This is known as a "flexible binding." When well done it results in a strong and handsome book. Since leather is the only material suitable for this style of binding, it is little used now except for very fine hand bindings. Directions will not be given here for this type of binding because it is quite beyond the skill of the average amateur and should not be undertaken without expert instruction.

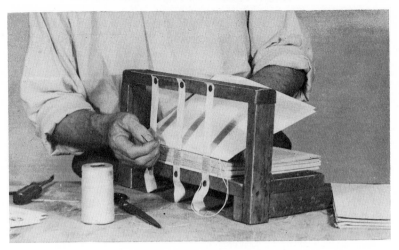

Fig. 23. Sewing.

1. Putting on tapes or cords. Place the stack of sections face down on the sewing frame, with the backs of the sections even with the front edge of the frame. If tapes are used, stretch them tightly in position between the saw cuts, fastening them at both ends with thumbtacks (Fig. 23).

Put the cords on exactly at the grooves. Tie a single knot in the lower end of the cord and push a thumbtack through it into the lower edge of the frame. Start a tack at the top, take a turn around it with the cord, and drive the tack in tight. Cut the cord and repeat.

2. Sewing on sections. Remove the book from the sewing frame and stack it face up on the table nearby. Thread a large needle with unbleached linen thread, but if it is not available, white cotton will do. If the book consists of only a few thick sections, the thread may be doubled. This not only increases the strength of the binding but gives the additional thickness needed at the back for backing.

The end papers may be sewed as the other sections are, or they may be tipped on with paste after the sewing is completed. Some binders prefer not to sew the end papers, so that the thread will not show at the accordion pleat. If end papers are to be sewed on, open each at the accordion pleat and, with a sharp awl or needle, punch a hole through the hinge at each mark, to correspond with the saw cuts.

To begin sewing, place the first section face down on the sewing frame, and hold the pages open at the accordion pleat with the left

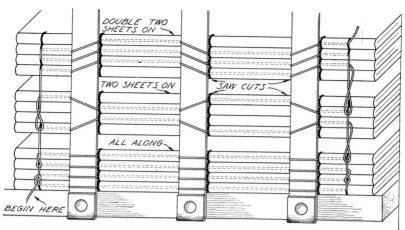

Fig. 24.   Methods of Sewing.

hand (Fig. 23). Insert the needle at the first (left) saw cut, carry it inside the section with the left hand to the next hole where it is passed out, eye end first, then carried around the tape and in at the next hole, and so on, to the end of the sheet. Pull the thread through until 3 or 4 inches are left at the starting hole. Drop the leaves of the first section, and put the next section in place, face down. Note that the head will be at the right. This second section is opened at the center and sewed onto the tapes as was the first, starting at the right end where the first section was finished. Pull the thread tight through this section and tie it to the end left out at the beginning. This ties the first two sections together at both ends. Put the next section in place and sew back through it to the opposite end. In every case be careful to have the section open at the exact center, and to have all sections in their proper order and facing the same way.

Cords are sewed on exactly the same way, except that the needle re-enters the same hole, after passing around the cord. The method of sewing just described is known as "all along" (Fig. 24).

Another method sometimes used for thick books consisting of many thin sections is "two sheets on" sewing. This technique is used to prevent excessive thickness at the back (Fig. 24). In sewing a book by this method, sew the first three or four sections "all along." Then put the next section in place and start the sewing as usual. After sewing to the first tape or cord, put another section in place and insert the needle in it after crossing the first tape or cord. Bring the needle out at the next tape or cord, across it, and back into the first

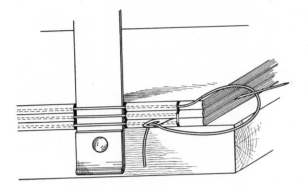

Fig. 25.
Kettle Stitching.

section, and so on, alternating between the sections to the kettle stitch. This style of sewing, while not as strong as the "all along" style, sews on two sections with one thread, thus reducing the thickness at the back. It is not recommended for general use. Sew the last three or four sections "all along."

A method of sewing giving still greater strength than the "all along" method is the "double two sheets on" method (Fig. 24). In this method each section is sewed "two sheets on" with the preceding section. Thus each section is sewed to the sections above and below it, giving greater holding power than "all along" sewing, for two threads pass through each section and the breaking of one will not release the section.

3. Kettle stitching. After sewing the third section, kettle stitch it at the end as shown in Figure 25. This consists of passing the needle behind the thread joining the two preceding sections and bringing it up through the loop thus formed. When pulled tight it

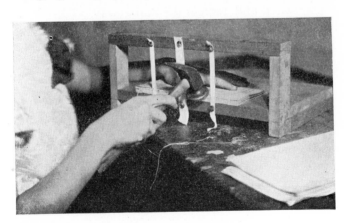

Fig. 26.
Knocking Down
the Sections.

Fig. 27.
Book Sewed
on Cards.

forms a knot and holds the ends of the sections together. It should be done after sewing each section. After sewing the final section, sew the second end paper, and take several kettle stitches to secure the end of the thread.

4. Starting a new thread. When the first thread gives out, leave its end hanging out at the end of the last section, and start a new thread at the same end of the next section. Pull the new thread through the section and kettle stitch, leaving about 6 inches of thread hanging out. Pull the two loose ends up snugly and tie securely. Snip off the ends about ½ inch from the knot and proceed with sewing. If a thread breaks inside a section, the end should be pulled out and a new thread started as above.

5. Knocking down. While sewing, knock down every four or five sections between the tapes with the hammer, as shown in Figure 26. This prevents the back from swelling too much during the sewing process. On very thin books, this operation may be omitted, since extra thickness is needed for backing.

6. Taking the book from the sewing frame. Pull out the thumbtacks and remove the book from the frame. Trim the tapes or cords (Fig. 27) to leave about 2 inches extending on each side of the book. These projections are known as "slips."

Chapter 6 / Forwarding

THE steps that follow sewing, with the exception of end banding, are known as "forwarding." This carries the book through to "finishing" which includes stamping and decorating.

PASTING UP

When the book is clamped up for gluing, it is often difficult to keep the end sections in position. Pasting takes care of this, and strengthens the book at the end sections where it sometimes pulls apart (Fig. 28).

1. Pasting up front sections. Open the book between the end papers and the first section. Cover all of the top page except a ⅛-inch strip along the back or hinge edge. Spread paste along the uncovered edge. Remove the paste paper and close the book, being careful that the back and top edges of the sections are exactly even. Do the same between the next two or three sections.

2. Pasting up back sections. Turn the book over and paste up the last two or three sections as in step 1.

Fig. 28.
Pasting Up the
End Sections.

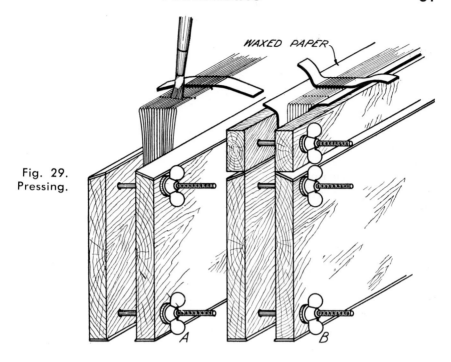

Fig. 29.
Pressing.

WAXED PAPER

3. Clamping up. Jog the back and head of the book up even and clamp lightly for a half hour or so.

GLUING UP

The beginner often finds it difficult to clamp up a thick book for gluing. The thickness at the back causes sections to slip out of place when pressure is applied. To overcome this, the method given here has been devised. When gluing up thin books it will probably not be necessary to use the sawing clamp. Simply slip the book all the way into the gluing press, leaving the back flush with or very slightly above the beveled edge of the press. With experience, modifications of the methods given here will suggest themselves.

1. Clamping for gluing. Jog the head and back of the book square and even. Clamp the book in the gluing press as shown at A, Figure 29, with 2 inches of the back projecting out of the press. Be sure the back is square or slightly rounded when the press is tightened, and that none of the sections have slipped in beyond or below the surface of the back.

Clamp up the exposed 2 inches of the book with the sawing

clamp, first putting a piece of waxed paper on each side of the book to keep the outside pages from sticking to the clamp. Since the lower part of the book is clamped in the gluing press, the sections will not slip out of place when the back is clamped. If the back is rounded slightly when clamped up tight, it will probably be about flat when the book is taken from the press. If clamped up perfectly flat, there is a tendency for it to be concave when taken from the press, making proper rounding difficult (B, Fig. 29).

After the sawing clamp has been tightened up with all sections in their proper position, loosen the wing nuts on the clamp a few turns to allow glue to work between the sections a very short distance.

2. Gluing. Thin a little hot or liquid glue to about half its usual thickness and spread it well over the back. Be careful that it does not run down too far between the sections.

3. Clamping the back. Tighten up the wing nuts on the sawing clamp. The back should be pressed in until it is only slightly thicker than the body of the book. Pull the tapes or cords tight across the back in order to remove the wrinkles that form in them when the back is pressed. If the wrinkles are not pulled out at this time, it will be impossible to do so after the glue has hardened.

When large books are clamped up, they tend to be thicker in the center because of the bending or springing of the sawing clamp. This can be overcome by the use of a large C clamp tightened across the back at the center.

CUTTING

The edges of a book after sewing usually are uneven and require trimming or cutting.

By "cutting" is meant cutting the edges from the head, tail, and fore edge of the book so as to make them perfectly smooth.

"Trimming" refers to cutting off only the higher sections, leaving the lower ones uncut. This is sometimes done in rebinding old books to improve their appearance without materially reducing their page size.

Books having antiquarian value should be trimmed very little if at all. They should preferably be very carefully sewed, pasted, and glued up, keeping the sections even at the edges, so that trimming will not be needed. If the book is clamped up and the edges are sanded with fine sandpaper, the book should be present-able without having its value impaired by cutting.

Bound volumes of magazines generally have to be cut, because of the difference in size of the numbers making up the volume. Of the several ways of cutting a book, the quickest and simplest is to use a printer's paper cutter. If a paper cutter is not available, a cutting press and plow can be made at small cost. It will not only answer the need for a cutter, but will at the same time provide firsthand experience with the method commonly used by craftsmen in the past, and to some extent in the present. This equipment makes possible an entirely satisfactory method of cutting, and is recom-mended for the beginner or amateur.

If neither a paper cutter nor the plow can be had, the edges can be cut by hand with a chisel. In some instances books are trimmed section by section before sewing, but this method is not recommended for beginners. Instructions for the three methods of cutting follow.

A. CUTTING ON A PRINTERS' PAPER CUTTER

When available, the paper cutter provides the quickest and easiest method of cutting. Generally one will be found in a school print shop or in some local commercial print shop where arrangements can be made for the trimming of the book.

1. Marking up. Square a trimming line across the head of the front end paper and the foot of the last end paper. The trimming line on the fore edge should be on the front.

2. Cutting the head. Lay the book face up with its back against the right-hand gauge of the cutter. Slip a piece of cardboard under the book. Because of the extra thickness at the back, it usually is necessary to build up under the book with a thickness or two of cardboard extending almost, but not quite, to the back. Build up the top in the same way, so that when the clamp is screwed down, the back will not be wrinkled and the sections forced out of place.

Set the back gauge of the cutter so the trimming line will come exactly under the front edge of the clamp when it is screwed down. Hold the back of the book tight against the right-hand gauge and screw down the clamp. Be sure the back is flat against the side gauge. Pull the operating lever, cutting the head of the book. It is important that the cut be from the back toward the fore edge to prevent the hinges from being torn or pulled out of shape.

3. Cutting the foot.   Turn the book over, and end for end. Bring the foot under the knife of the cutter, and the back against the right-hand gauge. Run the back gauge forward until the foot trimming line is under the edge of the clamp. Hold the back of the book tight against the side gauge and screw down the clamp. Take your time. Be sure the back and head are against the side and back gauges. It is difficult to correct crooked cutting. Cut as at the head.

4. Cutting the fore edge.   With the book face up and the head against the right-hand gauge, run up the back gauge until the trimming line is under the edge of the clamp. Hold the back of the book tightly against the back gauge and screw down the clamp. Be sure everything is square, and then cut.

B. CUTTING WITH THE PLOW

The use of the plow requires considerable care and skill, but when properly done results in a perfect cutting job. Since the plow and press are inexpensive to make and are so useful, they should be available to every amateur binder (Fig. 30).

Before beginning the cutting, see that the blade is sharp and set flush with the bottom of the plow. When sharpening, do not grind the bottom of the blade, because if it is not flat it will be impossible to cut a smooth, square edge.

1. Marking up.   Square a trimming line across the head of the

Fig. 30.   Cutting With the Plow and Cutting Press.

front end paper and across the foot of the last end paper. The trimming line on the fore edge should be on the front.

2. Guide boards. Cut two pieces of heavy cardboard or millboard about ½ inch larger each way than the pages of the book. With a little paste, stick one of these boards lightly on the front end paper with its top edge even with the trimming line at the head. Turn the book over and paste the other board on the back end paper with its edge even with the foot trimming line. These boards can be used later in making the covers for the book.

3. Clamping up. Slip a piece of waste cardboard in front of the backboard and clamp the book in the cutting press with the top edge of the front guideboard even with the top edge of the press. Be sure that the book is not twisted and that its back is straight and square in the press. If there is considerable extra thickness at the back, it may be necessary to block in with cardboard to prevent pinching the back.

4. Cutting the head. Set the plow on the press and adjust until the blade touches the book. Slide the plow back and forth, feeding the knife in a little before each forward stroke. Cut only on the forward strokes (from the back toward the fore edge) because an attempt to cut both ways will result in rough edges. Other causes of ragged cutting are a dull knife, loose clamping, and too much feed.

5. Cutting the foot. Remove the book from the press, turn it end for end, slip a piece of waste cardboard inside the front guideboard, and clamp up with the foot in position for cutting. Cut as above, being sure to cut from the back toward the fore edge.

6. Cutting the fore edge. Remove the book from the press, pull off the front guideboard and paste it on again even with the trimming line on the fore edge. Slip a piece of waste cardboard in front of the backboard, clamp up, and cut.

C. CUTTING WITH THE CHISEL

If no other equipment is available, a presentable cutting job can be done with a chisel (Fig. 31). A clamp or press similar to the gluing press will be needed, but both edges of the boards should be square and without the steel strips. The upper board may well be made thicker than the lower one to guide the chisel better. The lower board should be about 1 inch wider than the upper board,

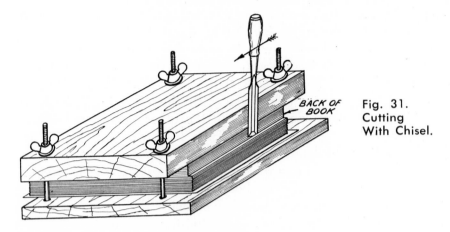

Fig. 31.
Cutting
With Chisel.

and the bolt holes so drilled that the extra width overhangs at one edge only.

1. Marking up.   Square a cutting line across the head on the front end paper and across the foot on the back end paper. The cutting line at the fore edge may be on either end paper.

2. Clamping up.   Clamp the book in the press with the head trimming line flush with the front edge of the top board. It will probably be necessary to block in under and on top of the book with cardboard to make up for the additional thickness at the back. Be sure the back of the book is straight and square when the clamp is tightened.

3. Cutting the head.   With a sharp chisel (about 1 inch wide) held flat against the edge of the top board, take slicing cuts along the cutting line, cutting from the back toward the fore edge. Tip the chisel slightly backward, as shown in Figure 31. Continue until the edge is completely cut.

4. Cutting the foot and fore edge.   The foot and fore edge are next cut in exactly the same way. In cutting the foot be sure to cut from the back to the fore edge.

ROUNDING

While a flat-back book opens better than one that has been rounded, it is not as nice in appearance and it has a tendency to cave in at the back after use. This is particularly true of thick or heavy books. For this reason rounding is an important step and should be carefully done. Carelessness in this step cannot be corrected later.

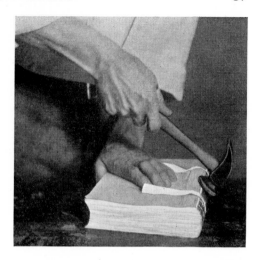

Fig. 32.
Rounding.

1. Softening the back. Moisten the glue on the back of the book with a wet cloth and give it a few minutes to soften.

2. Rounding. Lay the book on its side on the bench, with the fore edge toward you (Fig. 32). With the thumb of the left hand against the middle of the fore edge, and the fingers on top, pull toward you on the top pages, at the same time hammering lightly along the upper edge of the back with a backing hammer. A shoemakers' hammer can be used for this operation and for backing, which is the next step. Strike light, glancing blows, driving the outer sections of the book toward the fore edge. Turn the book over and repeat, continuing until the back and fore edge of the book have been well rounded.

BACKING

Backing is another important step, for backing and rounding determine the shape of the book. The thread used in sewing adds extra thickness to the back of the book. In backing, this extra thickness is made use of to form a shoulder or overhang against which the boards fit.

1. Clamping up for backing. Clamp the book tightly in the gluing press, allowing the back to extend from $\frac{1}{16}$ to $\frac{1}{8}$ inch above the beveled edges of the press. The exact amount will depend on the thickness of the boards used. Be sure to tighten all four screws to keep the book from slipping down into the press.

If the lying press is to be used, fit backing boards along the sides

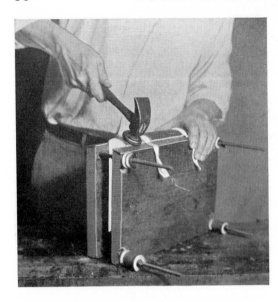

Fig. 33.
Backing.

of the book with their upper beveled edges so placed as to leave the proper margin to be hammered over. Lower the book and boards into the press and clamp up very tightly.

2. Backing. With the backing hammer, work along the back, striking light blows glancing toward the outside (Fig. 33). Work from the center toward the outside until the projection is hammered over to form a ledge. Backing must be done carefully, because careless hammering may cut the threads or tapes and ruin the book.

HEADBANDS

Headbands were formerly made by lacing a strip of catgut, cord, or leather into place at each end of the back. When properly put on, they add to the strength of the book as well as to its appearance, but of late years such headbands are used on only the most expensive hand-bound books. On factory-bound books, headbands are either omitted or consist of woven strips of cloth with a cord in one edge, glued into place on the ends of the back. When so made, the headbands cover the back edge of the sections and give a finished appearance to the book. Such headbands may be bought ready-made, or they may be made up as directed in this section. The exact stage at which headbands are put on is not important. They may be put on at this point or after the super is applied (see step 3 in Reinforcing

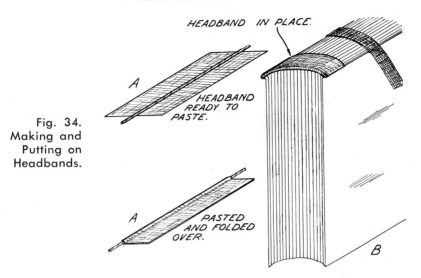

Fig. 34.
Making and
Putting on
Headbands.

the Back, following), but they should be put on before the back is covered (see step 4, following).

1. Making the headbands. Cut a piece of cloth about 1 inch wide and a little more than twice the width of the back in length. Its color should harmonize with the cover material to be used. Spread paste or glue on the wrong side of the cloth and stretch a piece of cord down the center lengthwise (A, Fig. 34). Fold the cloth together

Fig. 35.
Putting on
Headbands.

over the cord, press the cloth down alongside the cord with a folder, and let it dry (A, Fig. 34).

2. Putting on the headbands. Cut the headband just made into two lengths, each just long enough to fit over the back of the book. With the book still in the press, spread glue on about a half inch of each end of the back and press the headbands in place. Let the cord overhang the end of the back, press it down until it is flush on the back, and then let it dry. The headband is shown in place at B, Figure 34, and Figure 35.

REINFORCING THE BACK

The backs of books are commonly reinforced with "super," a loosely woven, heavily starched cotton cloth. For books which are to be given hard usage, a heavier material such as backing flannel should be selected. If this is not available, any strong cotton cloth will do, ranging in weight from cheesecloth for small books, to light canvas or duck for large, heavy books such as dictionaries and lawbooks. Regardless of the type of backing cloth that is used, it will be referred to as super in the following discussion.

1. Cutting the super to size. Cut the super equal in length to the distance between headbands, or about 1 inch shorter than the book, and 4 inches wider than the width of the back.

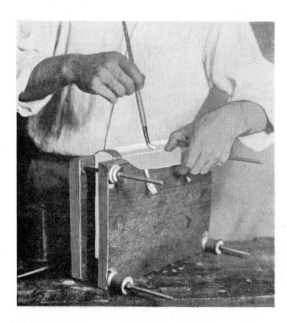

Fig. 36.
Pasting Down
Back Reinforcing.

2. Gluing up for the super. With the book still in the press, glue up the back thoroughly from end to end. Use fresh hot hide glue, liquid glue, or good padding cement.

3. Applying the super. Lay the piece of super in place on the back, overhanging about 2 inches on each side. Stretch the cloth in all directions and rub it well into the glue over the entire back (Fig. 36). If backing flannel is used, apply it with the nap side down, or next to the book.

4. Covering the back. Glue a piece of heavy paper down the back over the super to strengthen the back and cover up irregularities.

Fig. 37.
Pasting Down
the Slips.

Fig. 38.
Pasting Down
the Ends of Super.

GLUING DOWN THE SLIPS AND SUPER

1. Fraying out the slips.   This step will apply only to the use of cords, although the projecting ends of both tapes and cords are called "slips."

Untwist and fray the ends of the cords, fanning them out as much as possible.

2. Gluing down.   Spread the glue or paste under the slips and press them down on the outside end paper (Fig. 37). Then spread glue over the slips (Fig. 38) and on a 2-inch strip along the back edge of the end paper, and press down the projecting 2 inches of super. Use very little glue along the hinge so as not to stiffen the super and slips. Turn the book over and repeat this step.

3. Clamping up.   Wrap a piece of waxed paper over the back of the book to cover the fresh glue and clamp it in the press again to dry. Before clamping it is well to slip a piece of waxed paper or a tin plate between the outside leaves on each side of the book to keep the moisture of the glue from working into the book.

BOOKS TO BE CASED

If the book is to be cased, omit the rest of the operations in this chapter and continue with Casing, Chapter 7, or Removing and Repairing the Case in Chapter 8, depending on whether you are making a new case or repairing and replacing an old one.

MAKING THE BOARDS

Boards may be either single or double. If a good hard cover board is available, single boards will be adequate for all but the largest books, and are much simpler to apply. Cardboard or tablet backs should be doubled to give strength and stiffness.

1. Cutting the boards.   For single boards cut two pieces of board, and for double boards cut four pieces, each about ½ inch greater in length and width than the pages of the book. For double covers, two of the pieces may be millboard and the other two of thinner cardboard or strawboard.

The following steps apply only to double boards.

2. Marking and pasting.   Draw a line 2 inches from one edge of each board, and spread paste over all but the 2-inch strip on one side of each board.

3. Clamping up the boards. Put the boards together in pairs, with the pasted sides toward each other. If light and heavy boards are used, have one light and one heavy board in each pair. Place the light board next to the book and the heavy one on the outside. Clamp the boards in the press to dry.

BOARDING

The case or cover of a machine made book is made up completely and then pasted on the book. Such a book is known as a "cased" book. The hand binder has traditionally put the boards on the book before covering it, due originally to the practice of lacing the cords into holes punched in the boards. Whether tape or cords are used, the process of first boarding the book and then covering it is recommended for the beginner. This makes it possible for him to compensate for irregularities in assembling and cutting the book. On the other hand, casing is faster and in some ways simpler. It will be discussed later.

1. Preparing the book for boards. If single boards are to be used, or if the book is to be cased, it is now ready for that process. If double boards are to be used, the end sheet on both sides of the book should be trimmed about 2 inches from the back and 1 inch from the head and tail of the book. This leaves a tab consisting of the pasted-down ends of the tapes and super on each side of the book (Fig. 39).

2. Marking up the boards. Mark one of the boards "Front" and the other "Back." Place the one marked "Front" on the front of the book, leaving a space of about $\frac{1}{16}$ inch between the board and the ledge formed in backing the book. With double boards, slip the tab into the unglued 2-inch strip between the two halves of the board.

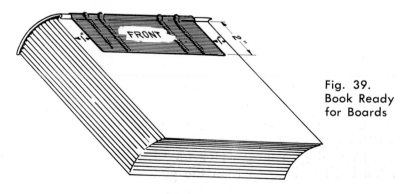

Fig. 39.
Book Ready
for Boards

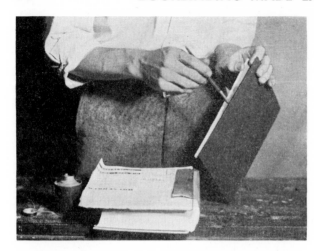

Fig. 40.
Gluing Up
Double Boards.

Holding the board in place, turn the book over and mark around it on the inside face of the board. Place the backboard in position, and repeat.

3. Marking for cutting. The overhang or "squares" of the boards should be the same at the head, the tail, and the fore edge, or they may be slightly larger at the tail. The exact amount will depend on the size of the book and the type of binding. For most books ⅛ inch will be enough. Assuming that it is to be ⅛ inch, draw a line that distance outside of and parallel to the outlines drawn on the boards.

4. Cutting the boards. Trim the boards along these outside lines, using a paper cutter, the plow and cutting press, or a sharp knife and steel square.

5. Fitting the boards. Fit the boards back on the book and see that the squares have been correctly cut.

5. Gluing on the boards. Remove the boards and slip a paste paper between the first two end sheets, or between the tab and the next end sheet, if the tab has been cut to insert double boards. Spread paste over the first end sheet, paying special attention to the pasted down super and tabs. Fit the front board in place, adjusting the squares carefully. If double boards are being used, paste up the tab, pry open the 2-inch unpasted strip at the back of the boards, and paste it thoroughly (Fig. 40). Then slip the tab into place between the boards and adjust the squares.

7. Clamping up. Slip a tin plate or waxed paper between each board and the book and clamp it in the gluing press.

COVERING THE BOOK

Many different materials as well as many combinations of materials are used in covering books. Formerly leather was used almost exclusively for good bindings, but due to its cost it is little used today except for the most expensive books. For the amateur, leather has the disadvantage of being difficult to handle properly, so leather bindings should not be attempted without personal instruction. Because of this, leather binding will not be discussed here. Those wishing information about it are referred to the books listed in the Bibliography.

The materials most readily available for book covers are paper, cloth, fabrikoid, and leatherette. Your choice of material will depend on the type of book, the cost of the material, and convenience with which it can be obtained. Attractive cover paper as well as some of the fabrics mentioned are carried by any local printer or paper supply house. Buckram, fabrikoid, and leatherette usually can be obtained only from professional binders, library supply houses, and arts-and-crafts supply houses.

If the book is to be "full bound," it is completely covered with one piece of material; for "half-bound" books the boards are covered with separate pieces of cloth or paper while another piece covers the back. The corners of a half-bound book may be protected with the material used on the back. The method of putting on a half binding follows.

A. HALF BINDING

1. Cutting the material. Cut two pieces of cover paper or cloth, each about 2 inches longer and 1 inch wider than the boards. In the following steps, this is referred to as "paper" to distinguish it from the material used on the back, but, of course, it may be cloth or any other cover material.

2. Fitting paper to the boards. Place the book with its back against a block of wood or another book of about its own thickness. Lay a piece of the cover paper face down on the block and turn the upper board back over it, as shown at A, Figure 41. Adjust the paper flush at the back edge of the board, with a 1-inch overhang at the head, the foot, and the fore edge. Bend this overhang up over the edges of the boards, creasing the paper at the bends.

3. Pasting up. Turn the cover board back over the book and spread paste evenly over the cover paper. Then swing the cover

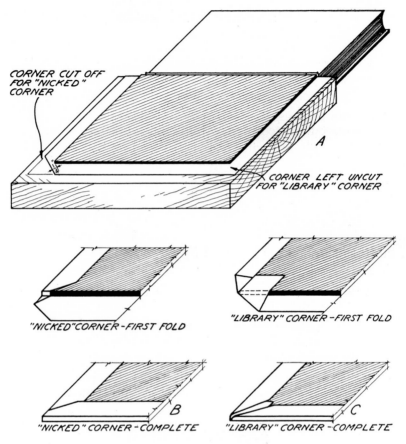

CORNER CUT OFF
FOR "NICKED"
CORNER

A

CORNER LEFT UNCUT
FOR "LIBRARY" CORNER

"NICKED" CORNER - FIRST FOLD

"LIBRARY" CORNER - FIRST FOLD

B

"NICKED" CORNER - COMPLETE

C

"LIBRARY" CORNER - COMPLETE

Fig. 41.   Covering Boards.

board back into place on the pasted paper. With a scissors, cut off the outside corners diagonally about ¼ inch from the corner of the board, as shown at A, Figure 41. Bring the pasted overhang at both ends up over the edge and press down on the inside of the board. Be sure the paper is pulled up tightly and that it fits snugly around the edges of the board. The corner is then "nicked in," as shown at B, Figure 41. To do this, press down the paper overhanging the corners with a paper knife or a folder. Then fold up the fore edge as was done at the ends. Lay a piece of waxed paper or tin plate on the end paper and close the book.

Another type of corner, the "library corner," is shown at C, Figure 41. In this binding, do not cut off the corners of the paper, but fold them over the corners of the board. Then fold up the ends and the fore edge, as shown at C, Figure 41.

Turn the book over and cover the other board in the same way.

4. Pressing. Cover each side of the book with tin plates or waxed paper, and place a tin plate or piece of waxed paper between the boards and end papers. Then clamp the book in a gluing press.

5. Trimming cover paper. When the paste is dry, remove the book from the press. Swing open the boards and, with a sharp knife or razor blade, cut through the paper about ⅜ inch from the edges on the inside of the boards. Carefully peel off the trimmed edges of the paper.

6. Padding the back. Cut a piece of kraft or drawing paper the length of the book and three times the width of the back. Fold this twice to make a three-ply strip or tube the width of the back of the book. Glue the center section to the back of the book. When the glue is dry, split the folded edges about an inch on each end.

7. Cutting material for the back. Cut a piece of material for the back, about 1½ to 2 inches longer than the boards and wide enough to cover the back of the book and come down about 1 inch on each side, or more if desired. The exact width will depend on the size of the book, the material, and the effect desired. This material is referred to as "cloth" in the following steps, but it should be understood that the same steps will be followed in the use of any fabric.

Fig. 42.   Tucking in the Ends of a Half Binding or Rebacking.

8. Pasting up the back.   Lay the cloth, wrong side up, on a piece of wastepaper, draw a pencil line down the center, and spread paste completely over it.

9. Covering the back.   Set the back of the book in the exact center of the pasted cloth, using the pencil line down the center as a guide. Pull up the edges of the cloth against the sides of the book. Turn the book so one end faces you, drop the boards, and have a helper hold the body of the book upright. Bring up the strip of cloth overhanging the end, slip it through the space between the boards and the back and into the slits in the folded tube pasted on the back. Tuck the end of the cloth into the back and press the corners well on the inside of the boards (Fig. 42).

Turn the book end for end and turn in the other end in the same way.

10. Clamping up.   Put a piece of waxed paper or tin plate inside the covers. Wrap another piece of waxed paper over the back of the book. Clamp the book in the gluing press in such a way that the overhanging metal edges form a groove between the back edge of the boards and the ledge formed when the book was backed. Do this clamping with care, for the appearance of the book depends largely on the groove along the back. Let it dry.

11. Trimming the back strip.   Remove the book from the press, swing open the boards, and with a sharp knife or razor blade trim the overlapping, turned-in ends of the back strip even with the trimmed edges of the cover paper, or about ⅜ inch from the head and foot.

12. Lining the boards.   Cut two pieces of heavy paper to fit exactly inside the trimmed edges of the boards and paste them down smoothly. This will make the inside of the covers smooth under the board papers and tend to counteract any warping of the boards due to pasting cover material on the outside.

13. Pasting down the board papers.   Open one cover and slip a paste paper under the first end paper or board paper. This will be the first colored or fancy sheet. Spread paste evenly over this sheet and close down the cover. Lift up the cover again and see that the sheet is evenly pasted to the board and lining. Smooth out any wrinkles, turn the book over, and repeat this step on the other cover.

14. Pressing.   Place waxed paper or tin plates inside the covers and again clamp up the book to dry.

Fig. 43.
Putting on a
Full Binding.

B. FULL BINDING

1. Cutting out the cover. Open the book wide, mark and cut a piece of cloth large enough to cover the book, with about ¾ to 1-inch margin on all edges. This will make the cloth about 2 inches larger in length and width than the wide-opened book.

2. Padding the back. (See step 6 in A. Half Binding in this chapter.)

3. Marking and pasting the back. Spread the cover cloth face down on a paste paper, and draw a pencil mark down the center of the back as an aid in centering the book on the cover. Spread paste evenly over the entire cloth, using a wide brush and working quickly.

4. Putting on the cloth. Set the back of the book on the center line of the cloth and lift the two sides up against the boards (Fig. 43). Turn the book so one end faces you, drop the boards, and have a helper hold the body of the book upright. Bring up the overhanging cloth at the center and tuck it into the back between the slits in the padding, as directed in step 9 in A. Half Binding. Fold over the margin along the end of the boards. Now turn the book end for end, and turn in the margin at the other end. Then turn in the margin at the fore edge, using one of the corners described in step 3, A, and shown in Figure 41.

5. Clamping up. (See step 10, A. Half Binding.)

6. Trimming the edges of cover cloth. (See step 5, A.)

7. Lining the boards. (See step 12, A.)

8. Pasting down end papers. (See step 13, A.)

9. Pressing. (See step 14, A.)

Chapter 7 / Casing

TODAY, for economical and fast production, books are machine sewed and cased, rather than being bound in the traditional hand manner. The case, consisting of the boards and their covering, is made up completely and then attached to the book as a unit.

Casing has both advantages and disadvantages for the amateur binder. Its advantages are: (1) the boards can be covered more easily when off the book; and (2) a helper is not needed to hold the book while the cover is applied, as in Figure 42.

The principal disadvantage of casing is the necessity for considerable accuracy in cutting, gluing, and backing the book, and in determining the proper dimensions of the case. A slight unevenness in pressure when gluing up, or an unnoticed twist in the book when cutting, may cause the spine to be wider at one end than the other, or the front or back of the book to be slightly larger or perhaps not quite square. These defects should be avoided, yet they do happen now and then. If the book is boarded before covering, the boards can be cut individually and fitted so as to make allowances for these irregularities. After the cloth is put on they will hardly be noticed. On the other hand, unless a book is very nearly perfect in make-up and dimensions, it is difficult to make a case that will fit properly.

The steps that follow are used for a full binding, but they may be easily modified for a half binding.

MAKING THE CASE

1. Cutting the boards. Cut two single boards ¼ inch longer than the book and ⅛ inch narrower than the measurement from the back edge to the fore edge. This measurement may be made immediately after the book is cut and before backing.

2. Cutting the cover cloth. With the book opened wide, mark and cut a piece of cover cloth large enough to cover the book with a

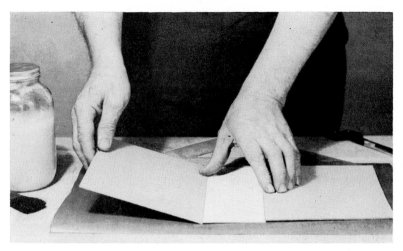

Fig. 44.   Lining Up the Boards With a Straightedge.

1-inch margin on all edges. This will make the cloth two inches longer and wider than the wide opened book.

3. Making the spacer.   Measure carefully across the spine of the book from one edge to the other. Cut a piece of cardboard equal in length to the length of the boards, and equal in width to the width of the spine plus ⅝ inch. NOTE: This is an important measurement, for it determines whether or not the overhang on the fore edge will be correct. After making and fitting your first case, you may want to modify this measurement in the future to obtain the correct overhang.

4. Making the lining for the back.   Cut a piece of kraft or drawing paper the length of the book and three times the width of the spine. Fold this twice to make a three-ply strip or tube. Split the folded edges about an inch from each end.

5. Pasting up the back.   Lay the cloth, wrong side up, on a piece of wastepaper. Arrange the boards, with the spacer between them, in the center of the cloth. Line them up carefully with a straightedge (Fig. 44). Now lift one of the boards, turn it over on another piece of wastepaper, and spread paste over it. Turn it paste side down again and return it to its position on the cloth, being careful to fit it against the straightedge and spacer. Press it down well and repeat the process with the other board.

6. Lining the back.   Remove the spacer, spread paste on the center section of the three-ply liner made in step 4, and press it in place exactly between the two boards.

Fig. 45.   Applying Paste to the Cloth.

7. Checking the squares.   At this stage you can fold the partially completed case around the book and see how well it is going to fit. If the overhang at the fore edge is too large or too small, it can be adjusted by taking up the boards and moving them in or out as the occasion demands. With experience, you should be able to gain confidence in your measurements and omit this step.

8. Cording the ends.   (This step is not absolutely necessary and may very well be omitted on small books.) Cut two pieces of cord equal in length to the distance between the two boards, rub them with paste, and lay them in position at the ends of the liner (Fig. 45).

9. Making the corners.   To make nicked corners, cut off the corners of the cover cloth ¼ inch from the corners of the boards (A, Fig. 41). To make library corners, paste the cloth around the corners and turn in all four corners.

10. Pasting the edges.   Paste the cloth along the two outside edges of the case and turn in (Fig. 45). Paste the cloth along the ends and turn in, folding the cloth over the boards and slipping the folded edge through the slit ends of the back liner. This leaves two thicknesses of paper between the folded edge and the back.

11. Scoring the back.   Turn the case over, rub the cloth down well on the boards, and score or crease along the inside edges of the boards with a folder. This helps form the crease along the back when the case is put on the book.

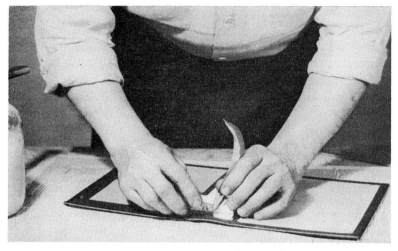

Fig. 46. Trimming the Cloth

12. Drying the case. Stack some heavy books or magazines on the case and leave to dry.

13. Trimming the case. When dry, turn the case inside up and with a razor blade and straightedge trim the edges of the cloth about ½ inch from the outside edges. Where the cloth extends beyond the ends of the back liner it may be trimmed as shown in Figure 46.

Fig. 47. Pasting the First Flyleaf.

PUTTING ON THE CASE

At this point you learn how well your case fits the book. If your measurements are correct and you checked the squares as suggested in step 7 of this chapter, the case should fit perfectly.

1. Fitting the case. Fold the case around the book (see Gluing Down the Slips and Super in Chapter 6). Adjust the squares so as to obtain a uniform overhang on all edges.

2. Pasting. Lay the book, face up, on the bench. Turn back the front cover and insert a paste paper under the first flyleaf. Spread paste over the flyleaf, giving special attention to the pasted down slips and super (Fig. 47). Swing the front cover back in place, being careful to pull the back up tight as you do so. See that the squares are uniform. Turn the book over and repeat with the back cover.

3. Pressing the book. Slip a tin plate inside each cover and clamp the book in the gluing press with the overhanging metal edges forming the groove along the back edge of the boards. Do this carefully to insure an even groove and a neat job.

Chapter 8

Repairing Books

MANY books are so poorly bound that they loosen up and fall apart after very little use because of cheap construction and material. Libraries, therefore, frequently buy books as printed sheets and have them bound at binderies that make a business of turning out strong and substantial books. The public cannot do this, however, and so books with contents well worth preserving often are hardly usable because of poor binding. If these books are rebound while the sewing is still good, the process is much simpler and quicker, since a number of steps may be omitted. If the sewing has been broken or pulled out, the book should be completely rebound as directed in the preceding operations.

When rebinding a book it is desirable to use the old case if possible. This is particularly true of antique books, or those having sentimental value. If the old case is to be used, the book should not be cut, for cutting will cause too much overhang at the edges. This means

Fig. 48.
Cutting Away
the Case.

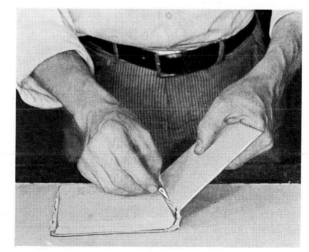

that the book must be very carefully sewed and glued, so as to keep the edges even and make cutting unnecessary.

The steps to be taken in rebinding without resewing, or in putting the old cover on a resewed book, are as follows. This method may also be used for putting board covers on paper-covered pamphlets or books.

REMOVING AND REPAIRING THE CASE

1. Removing the case. With shears, a sharp knife, or a razor blade, cut along the sides of the back, cutting through the super or reinforcing cloth (Fig. 48). If the contents already are completely out of the case, this step will not be necessary.

2. Stripping the case. Pull off the strips of super and loose lining paper along the inside surfaces of the boards. Carefully pull and scrape off all paper along the inside back edges of the boards. If the paper lining in the back is worn or loose, remove it.

3. Repairing the case. Paste down any loose or torn areas of the cover cloth. If the back is not too badly worn, a piece of cloth of similar color pasted inside will add strength without being noticeable. This is especially advisable in the case of antique books. If the back is badly worn or torn, it may be more desirable to reback it as directed in Rebacking the Case following.

4. Replacing back lining. Cut a piece of kraft or drawing paper or any other heavy paper that will just fit into the back, or make it the size of the old lining just removed. Spread paste over this lining and fit it into place in the back, slipping the ends under the folded cover cloth. Rub down with a folder.

REBACKING THE CASE

If the back of the case is badly torn it should be recovered with a strip of cover cloth or fabrikoid. If the back is completely gone and the boards are off the book, the case should not be rebacked before it is put on the book. Instead, the boards should be pasted on and the backing put on as directed in Half Binding in Chapter 6.

The following steps are to be observed when the fabric joining the boards at the back is sufficiently intact to hold them apart at the proper distance.

1. Cutting cloth for the back. Lay the case flat on the bench to

Fig. 49.
Rebacking
the Case.

measure. Cut a piece of cover cloth 2 inches longer than the boards and about 2 inches wider than the space between them.

2. Pasting and placing the back strip. Spread paste evenly over the inside of the cloth strip. With the case spread out flat, outside up, on a paste paper, stretch the pasted strip down the center. Adjust the strip so as to have the same lap on both boards, rub it down, and wipe off any excess paste that may have squeezed out (Fig. 49).

3. Lining the back. Cut a piece of heavy paper the length of the boards and just wide enough to fit the space between them. Turn the case over and fit this paper in between the boards.

4. Folding down the ends of the back strip. Fold in and rub down the ends of the back strip. Wipe off excess paste.

5. Scoring the case. Turn the outside of the case up again and

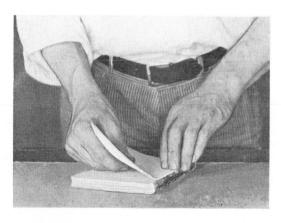

Fig. 50.
Putting on
End Papers.

crease or score along the inside (back) edges of the boards with a folder. This helps to form the crease along the back when the case is put on the book.

PREPARING CONTENTS FOR BINDING

1. Removing the super and glue. Pull off the old super and scrape off any glue that still adheres to the back. If the glue is hard, moisten it with a wet cloth before attempting to pull off the super. Be very careful not to break or pull out the stitches.

2. Making end papers. Make up and assemble end papers as directed in Making End Papers in Chapter 5. Two-leaf end papers made from a single folded sheet usually are sufficient.

3. Pasting on end papers. Spread paste ¼ inch wide along the back edge of the end papers. Place them in position with the pasted edge even with the back of the book (Fig. 50), rub down and let it dry.

PUTTING ON THE SUPER AND HEADBANDS

Since the book has not been pulled apart, it should not be necessary to round or back it. Clamp it up in the gluing press as for backing, and apply super as directed in Reinforcing the Back in Chapter 6. If headbands are desired, apply them as directed in Headbands in Chapter 6.

PUTTING ON THE CASE

1. Trimming end papers. With a pair of shears trim the end papers even with the edges of the book (Fig. 51).

2. Pasting up. Lay the book on the bench, and slip a paste paper

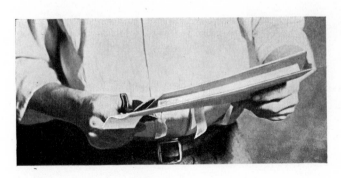

Fig. 51.
Trimming
End Papers.

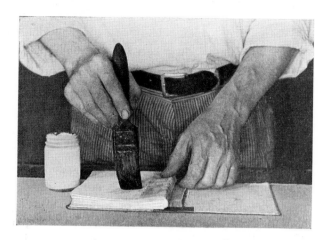

Fig. 52.
Pasting Up
for Recasing.

under the front end paper or board paper. Spread paste evenly over the board paper and glued-down super (Fig. 52).

3. Fitting the front board. Put the front board in place on the pasted board paper. Pick up the book and close the case around it. Turn it face down and adjust the squares.

4. Pasting and fitting the backboard. Lay the book face down, open the case, and paste up the last board paper as directed for the front. Close the case on the pasted board paper. Turn the book over and adjust the squares.

5. Pressing the book. Slip a tin plate or waxed paper inside each cover and clamp the book in the gluing press with the overhanging metal edges forming the groove along the back edge of the boards. Do this carefully to insure an even groove and a neat job.

Chapter 9
Binding Single Sheets

THE binder is occasionally called upon to bind a book of single sheets, such as typewritten or mimeographed material. This calls for a somewhat different procedure, but is not particularly difficult. Most large mail-order catalogs and telephone directories are made up from single sheets, which proves that single sheets can be bound successfully. They are cemented at the back and reinforced with a piece of open-weave cloth. While these books are not intended for long use, they wear very well considering the simplicity of their binding.

For the first step in binding a book of single sheets, place a piece of cardboard of sheet size on each side of the stack and jog it up square at the back and head. Clamp the book in the gluing press with the back flush with or slightly above the beveled edge of the press. Glue or cement the back thoroughly with fresh hot glue or good padding cement and leave to dry.

When dry, make up end papers and tip them on about 1⁄16 inch from the back, as described in Making End Papers in Chapter 5, first pulling off the two cards placed on the outside of the sheets when gluing.

If the edges are rough, cut the head, tail, and fore edge with a paper cutter or plow. If the sheets are of uniform size this may not be needed, but trim the end papers with a shears.

Clamp it again in the gluing press with the back edge exposed about 1⁄8 inch above the beveled edge. With a fine-toothed saw, such as a hack saw or backsaw, cut grooves across the back about 1⁄2 inch from each end and 1½ inches apart. Cut these grooves on a slant like the sides of an inverted V, two cuts being required for each groove,

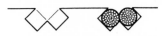

Fig. 53. Saw Cuts to Hold Cords When Binding Single Sheets.

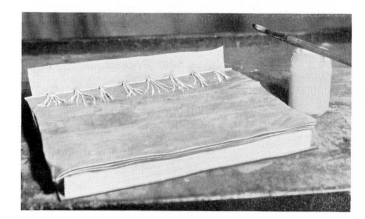

Fig. 54.
A Book of Single
Sheets With
Cords in Place.

as shown in Figure 53. Work the glue or cement into the grooves, and force a short length of cord into one side of the first cut, followed by another cord in the other side of the same cut. These two cords should fill the groove tightly, and on account of its dovetailed shape they should be securely held in place. Make the cords long enough to extend about 2 inches beyond the back on each side. Use any strong cord that frays out easily on the ends.

Fill all the saw cuts with cords in the same way (Fig. 54). Then take the book from the press and round it as directed in Rounding in Chapter 6. Return it to the press, clamp it up to the cords, and back it carefully with a backing hammer (see Backing in Chap. 6). Do

Fig. 55.
Frayed-Out Slips
With Super Ready
to Paste Down.

both the rounding and the backing immediately after the cords are put in the grooves and before the glue holding them has dried. Glue or cement the back thoroughly and put on a piece of super or other reinforcing cloth (see Reinforcing the Back in Chap. 6, and Fig. 55).

When dry, remove the book from the press, trim the ends of the cords to a uniform length of 1½ to 2 inches, and fray them out. Glue the frayed-out slips down flat on the end paper as shown in Figure 37. Glue down the super on top of the slips (Fig. 38). Wrap a waxed paper over the back and press until dry. Complete the binding as directed in Making the Boards, Boarding, and Covering the Book in Chapter 6.

There is another method of binding single sheets, which is somewhat better but at the same time more laborious. After the book is first glued as described above, mark and saw it for sewing on tapes, as directed in Sawing in Chapter 5. Then take it from the press and pull it apart into sections of eight or ten leaves. Next, carefully overcast the backs of these sections with fine thread, stitching them about ¾ inch apart and ⅛ inch from the back. Then sew the book and complete the binding as directed in Sewing in Chapter 5 and Chapter 6.

A quick and easy method of binding loose sheets, magazines, and pamphlets makes use of a drilling clamp, which may be purchased from library supply houses or made like the one shown in Figure 56.

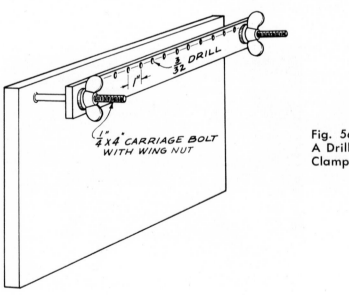

¼" × 4" CARRIAGE BOLT
WITH WING NUT

Fig. 56.
A Drilling
Clamp.

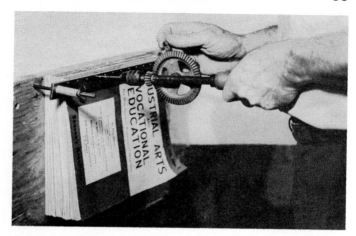

Fig. 57.
Drilling.

The length of the clamp depends on the size of the magazines to be bound. If it is made 16 inches long as shown, it can be used in magazines such as *Industrial Arts and Vocational Education*. With the aid of the clamp, holes are drilled through the book material about ⅛ inch from the back and the sewing goes through these holes. Books bound in this manner will not open flat, nor can they be rounded or backed successfully. However, if a quick and inexpensive method of preserving notes, papers, magazines, or pamphlets for occasional reference is needed, this one is quite satisfactory.

1. Drilling. Jog up the stack of magazines or notes even at the head and back. Clamp up flush with the top edge of the clamp bar. If you are binding thick single-section magazines, it may be necessary to push them a little higher in the clamp in order to be sure of drilling and sewing through the center pages. Now drill through each hole in the clamp and completely through the book using a ³⁄₃₂-inch drill (Fig. 57). Be careful to drill straight so the drill does not come out the back. If a bench drill is available, lay the clamp and book on the table of the drill and drill as above. This is really preferable, because the power drill is more likely to go straight through. When the drilling is complete, loosen the wing nuts and slip the book up in the clamp an inch or so. Then with the clamp and book sitting upright in the vise, proceed with the sewing.

2. Sewing. Use a heavy linen thread such as Hayes No. 16–4H, or if this is not available, use any strong cotton cord. Thread a long darning needle with about ten feet of thread, pull it through the eye of the needle to the center of the cord and double it, knotting the

Fig. 58.   Sewing.

two ends together. Now sew through the first hole from front to back, pulling the doubled thread through until about an inch of the knotted end protrudes. Pass the needle back to the front through the second hole, and through the knotted end of the thread. Then return it to the back through the second hole and pull the thread up tight. This will pull the knot into the second hole (Fig. 58). Then continue down the length of the book, sewing back and forth through succeeding holes and pulling the thread up tight as you proceed. When the opposite end is reached, sew back again in the same manner to the second hole, where the needle is passed under the beginning thread and the thread knotted securely. Note that you will have two doubled threads through each hole except the two end ones.

3. Cutting. The book may now be cut along the ends and fore edge by any of the methods already discussed.

4. Binding. As already mentioned, books sewed in this manner cannot be rounded or backed very well. However, if a finished binding is desired, end papers may be made up and tipped on, a piece of super or backing flannel glued over the back, and boards pasted on and covered, or a case made up and fitted to the book. If appearance is not important and the binding is only for the purpose of preserving the contents for occasional reference, a satisfactory case may be made by cutting a piece of heavy cover paper large enough to fold around the book, covering both sides and the back. Make two folds down the center just far enough apart to fit neatly over the back. Spread glue over the back of the book and fit the case on it. Stand it on its back to dry, with books or book ends on both sides to hold it up. When dry, the back may be lettered and the front decorated if desired.

Chapter 10  Finishing

IN THE bookbinder's language, finishing means the "stamping" and "decorating" of a book. Because of the necessary limitations of this book, little will be said of decoration beyond that given a book by a suitable title.

Much of the appearance of a book depends on its stamping. The commonest method of stamping has long involved the use of gold leaf, and when done by hand, it requires considerable equipment and skill. Because of this, it may be well for the beginner to forego this professional touch, and instead paste printed or hand-lettered paper labels on the backs of his books. A well-designed label with a neatly ruled border adds much to the appearance as well as to the usefulness of a book.

On the front cover of half-bound volumes of magazines, an appropriate decoration is one of the magazine covers. Full-bound volumes generally look better with the title on the back only, though that is, of course, a matter of personal preference.

Ordinary paste may be used for fastening labels to cloth or paper bindings, but on leatherette or fabrikoid a cement must be used.

Before taking up the subject of gold-leaf stamping, it might be well to mention that gold-leaf work is an art in itself, and the beginner should not expect perfect results on the first attempt. Much practice will be required, and first attempts should be made on scraps of cover material stretched over the rounded edge of a plank shaped to simulate the back of a book. Stamping a book should not be attempted until a passable job can be done on a practice piece. If possible, the student or home craftsman should visit a job bindery where books are hand lettered and decorated, to get a firsthand idea of how the work is done.

The printing and decorating on the books in any library will furnish a variety of ideas as to the arrangement and location of titles and decorations. During a visit to a school or public library, bound

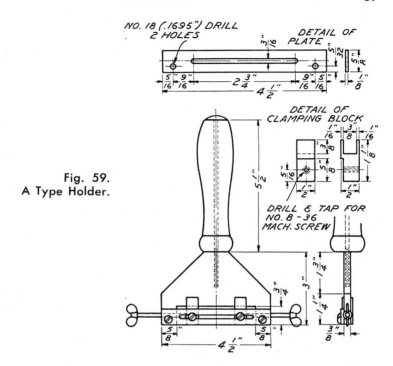

NO. 18 (.1695") DRILL
2 HOLES

DETAIL OF PLATE

DETAIL OF CLAMPING BLOCK

DRILL & TAP FOR NO. 8-36 MACH. SCREW

Fig. 59.
A Type Holder.

volumes of magazines which have been stamped also can be studied, and patterns of planned titles can be made with pencil and paper. The location and arrangement of lines often put at the head and the tail should be studied.

The minimum of equipment needed will include the following: a type holder, an assortment of type, a pallet or fillet, a heater, a gold cushion, a book of gold leaf, a small box of gilding powder, albumen, and a gold knife.

The type holder is rather expensive to buy and the most difficult to make. However, one can be made with only the ordinary hand tools for working metal, and at little cost. Details of one of the simplest forms are given in Figure 59. The commercial type holders make use of a single right- and left-hand screw, the two jaws moving in and out together. This is more desirable and is recommended as an interesting problem for those in a position to do more difficult machine work. Before attempting to build it, the maker should examine such a holder and see it in use.

While brass type is the best for stamping, foundry-cast lead type is perfectly satisfactory and will last a long time. Linotype slugs or

NUMBER OF CHARACTERS	A	B	C	D	E	F	G	H	I	J	K	L	M	N	O	P	Q	R	S	T	U
75	3	2	2	2	3	2	2	2	3	1	1	2	2	2	2	2	1	2	2	2	2
100	4	3	3	3	4	2	2	3	4	2	2	3	3	4	4	2	1	3	3	3	3
125	5	4	4	4	5	3	3	4	5	3	3	4	4	5	5	3	2	4	4	4	4
150	6	4	4	4	6	3	4	4	6	3	3	5	5	5	6	4	2	4	5	5	4
175	8	5	5	5	8	4	4	6	8	3	3	5	5	6	7	4	3	6	6	6	4

NUMBER OF CHARACTERS	V	W	X	Y	Z	&	.	,	'	-	1	2	3	4	5	6	7	8	9	0
75	2	1	2	1	1	1	2	1	1	1	1	2	2	2	2	2	2	2	2	2
100	2	2	2	2	1	1	3	3	2	1	2	2	2	2	2	2	2	2	2	2
125	3	2	3	2	1	1	1	4	3	2	2	2	2	2	2	2	2	2	2	2
150	3	3	3	3	2	2	4	4	2	2	3	3	3	3	3	3	3	3	3	3
175	4	4	4	3	2	2	6	5	2	2	3	3	3	3	3	3	3	3	3	3

monotype should not be used, for they are made of softer lead and will not stand the heat and pressure. A minimum of about 100 characters will serve for most titles, though a larger assortment may be needed at times. Capitals should be used throughout. For a first experiment it may be possible to buy, beg, or borrow the few pieces of type needed for one or two titles from a local printer or from the school printshop. If only one size can be had, 18 point is a good size to begin with. Any fairly bold face type will do. If a second font is added, it should be smaller, 12 or 14 point, or a larger, condensed type. In the following table, useful type assortments of from 75 to 175 characters are given.

A pallet or a fillet is used for making a line or lines across the head and the tail of the back. The pallet is easy to make, as shown in Figure 60. It is hack-sawed and filed from a piece of ¼-inch sheet brass or copper, and fitted with a wooden handle. A fillet

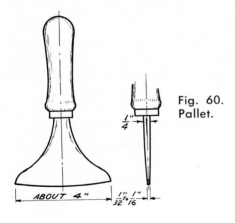

Fig. 60.
Pallet.

ABOUT 4"

consists of a brass disk fitted into a handle. It is used for lining the back and more particularly for lining or decorating the boards. For the simple stamping described here a fillet will not be needed.

The heater may be any small gas or electric plate, or a burner on the gas range may be used.

The gold cushion is made by covering the top of a board about 6 by 12 inches with a padding of cotton or folded paper, and a piece of soft leather, flesh side up. It must be free from oil or grease.

Gold leaf can be purchased in books of 25 sheets from binders' and sign painters' supply houses. The cost will vary with the quality and the price of gold. Stamping foil is thin plastic tape with sized metal leaf on one side. It is available in gold, aluminum, and imitation gold, as well as a variety of colors, and in various widths. While intended for use in stamping machines, this material may also be used with hand stamping equipment. It is easier to handle than unmounted gold leaf.

For a gold knife an ordinary kitchen table knife will do, but it must be free from oil or grease.

Gilding powder is put up in small as well as large quantities, and can be bought from binders' supply houses. It is used for holding the gold leaf to the leather or fabric when heat and pressure are applied.

Glair is used for the same purpose. It is made from the white of eggs or dried albumen. If it is made from the white of eggs, the egg white should be beaten with a half-teaspoonful of white vinegar, allowed to settle overnight, and strained off for use.

There are three general methods of applying gold leaf to books. In the first and simplest method for the amateur, the surface to be lettered is dusted with gilding powder, and the gold leaf is picked up on the type and struck in place. The second is the older method used and recommended by many hand binders. It consists of painting the parts to be decorated or lettered with one or two coats of glair. When dry, the gold leaf is placed in position, marked, and struck with the heated letters or tools.

The third method is that used in commercial binderies where the stamping is done on the case by machine before it is put on the book. It makes use of ready-sized gold leaf mounted on a paper ribbon. Though intended for machine operation where pressure and temperature can be controlled, it can be used by the amateur, and the steps will be described.

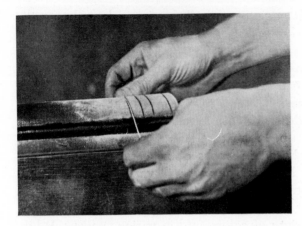

Fig. 61.
Guide Lines
for Lettering.

STAMPING WITH GILDING POWDER

1. Clamping up.   Clamp the book with the back up between two boards in a bench vise, in a glue press, or in a lying press. Clamp it close to the back to give good support, for considerable pressure must be used in lettering.

2. Sizing.   With a small wad of cotton dipped in gilding powder dust the parts that are to be lettered or lined.

3. Marking.   With a thread stretched between the hands make a mark through the gilding powder and across the back, just below each line of lettering, and each line at the head and tail (Fig. 61).

4. Preparing the gold leaf.   Gold leaf must be handled in a place free from drafts. Slip the knife under the first sheet in the book and lift it to the gold cushion. Breathe gently on the center to flatten it out. Do not touch it with the fingers or anything oily or greasy, because it will stick. Be sure the knife and cushion are free from grease. If you rub the cushion occasionally with a dry cake of Bon Ami or Sapolio the surface will be improved.

Cut the gold with the knife into strips a little wider than the type face, using a sawing motion. If lines are to be put on, cut some narrow strips for them.

5. Setting up.   Set up the type for the first line, and clamp the type tightly in the holder. If two of the lines are short words, save time by setting them up together with a space between them.

6. Heating.   Put the type holder and type on the heater and leave it until the moistened finger tip sizzles when touched to the type. The correct temperature will depend somewhat on the cover

Fig. 62.
Picking Up
Gold From Cushion.

material, and is best determined by experiment. To be on the safe side, do not get it too hot.

7. Lettering. After the holder and type are heated to the proper temperature, rub a small pad or rag slightly greased with petroleum jelly over the face of the type. This leaves a film of grease which

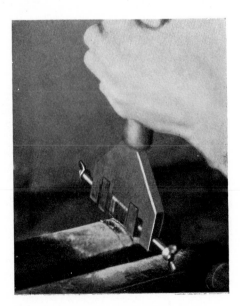

Fig. 63.
Lettering the Back.

will pick up the gold leaf. Set the line of type lightly on one end of the first strip of gold (Fig. 62). It will probably not use more than half the length of the strip, so lift it up and swing the remaining length under the type and pick it up in the same way. It will stick to the first layer of gold and make a double thickness, covering any cracks in the first layer and resulting in brighter and more solid letters.

Hold the type over the proper line on the book and center it. Then set one end down in place firmly, and slowly roll the line of type over the back of the book, using a firm, even pressure (Fig. 63). The amount of pressure will depend on the size of the type and the length of the line. It will be impossible to do good lettering if the back has not been well padded or is not well supported.

Wipe off any excess gold clinging to the type, reset for the next line, reheat, and repeat.

8. Lining. Heat the pallet, rub the edge over the pad with petroleum jelly on it, and pick up a narrow strip of gold leaf long enough to go across the back of the book. Since narrow strips are likely to be cracked when cut, pick up a double thickness of gold.

Carefully roll the edge of the pallet over the back of the book, and be sure to keep just above the guide line and to maintain an even pressure (Fig. 64). Since the edge of the pallet is narrow, the pressure should be less than when lettering.

Fig. 64.
Putting on Lines
With a Pallet.

9. Cleaning up. With a clean cloth wipe the surplus gold leaf and gilding powder from the back of the book.

STAMPING WITH GLAIR

Glair is somewhat more troublesome to use than gilding powder. It must be made up a day in advance and with its use the gold leaf is more difficult to handle, since it is picked up and placed on the book before stamping. The following steps cover the essentials.

1. Clamping up (see step 1 in Stamping with Gilding Powder).

2. Glairing. Dip a small wad of cotton in the glair and rub it evenly over the parts to be lettered or lined. Since the glair will show somewhat, try to confine it as much as possible to the parts to be stamped. Let it dry.

3. Marking up. With a pencil draw light lines across the back below each line of the title and decoration.

4. Preparing the gold leaf (see step 4 in Stamping with Gilding Powder).

5. Setting up (see step 5 in Stamping with Gilding Powder).

6. Heating (see step 6 in Stamping with Gilding Powder).

7. Greasing. When the glair is dry, rub over it very lightly with a wad of cotton dipped in petroleum jelly or coconut oil. For convenience place a spot of grease on the back of the left hand, and touch it with the wad of cotton when needed.

8. Applying the gold leaf. Make a small, tight wad of cotton, grease it very lightly, and with it pick up a strip of leaf. Carry it to its proper position on the book and pat it down lightly with a clean

Fig. 65.
Placing the
Gold on Glair.

wad of cotton (Fig. 65). Have just enough grease on the book to hold the gold, but not too much. If the gold is torn, breathe on it and place another piece over it.

9. Re-marking. Since the first marks were to serve only as a guide in placing the gold, which will have covered them up, it will be necessary to mark up the lines again. Mark lightly on the gold leaf with the point of a needle.

10. Stamping. If the type is too hot, cool it with a damp cloth until it just sizzles when touched with the moistened finger tip. Wipe the face of the type with a clean cloth, center the line, and make the impression, rocking slowly from one side of the back to the other. Do not try to rock back again, because it will be almost impossible to strike exactly the same places.

Wipe off the type, reset, reheat, and repeat on the next line.

11. Lining. With the pallet at the proper heat, rub its edges clean and roll it slowly over the back of the book at its proper mark. Be very careful to make the line straight and square.

12. Cleaning up. With a clean cloth wipe off excess gold and grease. If some of the gold sticks where it is not wanted, wash it off with a cloth dampened with benzine or high-test gasoline.

STAMPING WITH STAMPING FOIL

The use of stamping foil is probably the easiest method of applying gold. However, as with other methods, correct temperature and even pressure are most important. Considerable practice on waste material is recommended before stamping is attempted on a book.

1. Clamping up (see step 1 in Stamping with Gilding Powder).

2. Applying the foil. Cut a piece of foil long enough to go across the back of the book. Fasten it in place with the dull or metallic side next to the book, using a small piece of cellophane or masking tape at each end.

3. Marking up. With a ball point pen draw lines across the foil below each line of the title or decoration.

4. Setting up (see step 5 in Stamping with Gilding Powder).

5. Heating (see step 6 in Stamping with Gilding Powder).

6. Stamping. As in applying gold with glair or gilding powder, the proper temperature and even pressure are most important. Center the type and then roll it across the back of the book, starting at one end (Fig. 66). Do not attempt to roll back or repeat the stamping.

Fig. 66.
Stamping the
Foil.

7. Lining. Follow the same procedure as for lettering. The foil may be lifted and moved along the book for additional lines or lettering until all parts of the foil are used.

8. Cleaning up. Remove the foil and wipe the back of the book with a clean cloth.

Chapter 11 / The Book Bindery

IT IS only natural to expect that an age that has brought into being the many mass-produced objects of today's industry would also apply the principles of automation and the assembly line to bookbinding. In fact, it is only because of such modern methods that we are today able to buy books at a reasonable price. If books were still produced by hand methods, we would have a situation similar to that existing in the middle ages, when a single book lent distinction to its owner,

Fig. 67.
A Smyth
Sewing Machine.

Courtesy
John F. Cuneo Co.

and was beyond the reach of most. A library of a few hundred volumes could be owned only by noblemen and high church dignitaries. Today, because of the application of modern factory methods, fine volumes can be had at reasonable cost and libraries whose books number into the tens and hundreds of thousands are not unusual.

The modern book reaches the binder in the form of sheets printed on both sides, and usually with from eight to forty-eight pages on each sheet. These sheets are fed through an automatic folder which folds them into sections or signatures of the required size and with their pages in the proper order. If any illustrations or charts have been printed separately, they are tipped in at this stage by automatic machines or by hand.

After the sections are folded and stacked, they are taken to the gathering or collating machine where the stacks are placed in order in bins or hoppers. Arms carrying grippers remove them from the hoppers one by one and deposit them in order on a moving belt, assembling the sections of each book in their proper order.

The machine-made book is not sewed on cords or tapes; instead the sections are sewed together on an automatic machine capable of sewing as many as 5000 sections an hour (Fig. 67). It is in sewing that the machine process differs the most from hand methods. Without cords or tapes, the support of the machine-made book in its case depends on the strength of the glue, super, and end papers alone. The ultimate drying and flaking away of glue on the backs of such books leaves them with only the thread to hold them together, while the cords or tapes of the hand-sewn book add materially to its strength and life.

When the ability to withstand hard use is of more importance than the ability to open flat, books are sometimes "flat sewed" on special sewing machines. This is a process similar to that described in Chapter 9 for the binding of single sheets, and results in a strong but inflexible back.

After sewing, the next step is the first gluing. This is quickly done by passing the back or spine of the book over a roller carrying the glue, which penetrates between the sections and holds them in place during trimming and backing.

The book is next trimmed on three sides on an automatic machine and goes to the backing or forwarding machine. Here the book is rounded and backed, the super is applied, and then the back liner which carries the headbands is glued on. Here, machine operations

Fig. 68.　A Sheridan Casemaking Machine.

have replaced hand labor with great saving of time and cost and without loss in quality of work. In fact, the machine product can be expected to be more uniform in size and shape.

The book is now ready for its case, which is being manufactured by a parallel and equally automatic method. Figure 68 shows the Sheridan case maker, one type of case-making machine which takes a roll of cover cloth, applies the paste or glue, drops the boards and back liner in place, cuts the cloth to size allowing proper margins, trims the corners, folds over the edges, and finally runs the case through rollers to ensure a smooth surface.

Stamping or printing the case comes next, in gold, aluminum, black, or colors. This is usually done in one operation, on presses especially designed for the purpose.

The final step is "casing in," or fitting the book in its case. This is a semiautomatic process in which paste is applied to the end papers by rollers, after which the case is dropped in place and pressed down. After inspection to see that the squares are uniform, the books are stacked between pressing boards and put in a hydraulic press to dry.

This completes the process of manufacturing a book, as it is carried out in a modern bindery. It is essentially the same as the hand methods we have studied, except for the fact that in the factory process most of the work is done by machines. The fact that books can be so made in no way detracts from the pleasure and satisfaction to be derived from mastering the art of hand binding.

Glossary

This glossary is not intended as a complete list of bookbinding terms, but only of those more likely to be used by the beginner or amateur.

albumen. The white of egg used in preparing glair for gold-leaf lettering or decorating. It is also sold in dried form.

all along. The method of sewing books in which each section is completely sewed by itself.

backing. The forming of a groove or shoulder along the back of a book for the reception of cover boards.

backing boards. Wedge-shaped, bevel-edged boards used to hold a book while it is being backed.

backing hammer. A round-faced hammer used for backing and rounding, resembling a shoemaker's hammer.

band nippers. Pinchers with broad, flat jaws used for straightening bands and for nipping up the leather over raised bands after covering.

bands. Cords upon which the sections of a book are sewed in some types of binding.

blind tooling. Tooling or decoration put on without gold leaf.

board papers. The part of the end papers pasted to the boards.

bodkin. An awl used for making holes in the boards for slips.

bolt. The folded edge of a sheet in an uncut book.

boss. Raised metal ornament on the side of a book.

burnisher. A hand tool of steel, agate, or bloodstone set in a wooden handle, used for burnishing.

burnishing. Polishing or glazing a surface or edge with burnisher.

cased book. A book in which the book and cover are made separately, and the book is pasted into the finished case.

collating. Inspecting the sections to insure every page being in its proper place and right side up.

cord. A stranded hemp cord upon which books are sometimes sewed.

crinoline. A heavily starched, open-weave fabric, useful as a substitute for "super" in reinforcing book backs.

cutting boards. Wedge-shaped boards used in cutting the edges of a book with the plow and cutting press.

cutting in boards. The cutting or trimming of a book after the boards have been put on.

cutting press. A wooden screw press with a guide for the plow, used to hold books being cut with the plow. When turned over it becomes the "lying" press.

deckle edge. The rough, uneven edge of paper before cutting.

duodecimo. A section made up of a sheet folded into 12 leaves.

end papers. The extra leaves placed at the front and back of a book for appearance and protection.

featheredge. The beveled edge of a piece of leather.

fillet. A metal disk fitted with a handle, used to roll lines on book covers or backs.

finishing. The lettering or decoration on the cover of a book.

finishing press. A small adjustable press used to hold a book while it is being tooled or stamped.

flexible back. A method of binding in which the sections are sewed on raised cords with the threads looped around the cords.

folder. A flat piece of bone, ivory, or hardwood, shaped like a ruler or paper knife, used in folding sheets and other binding operations.

folio. A sheet folded once into two leaves or four pages.

fore edge. The front edge of a book, section, or page.

foot. The lower or bottom edge of a book.

forwarding. The steps between sewing and finishing, with the exception of headbanding.

gathering. Collecting together the sections to make up a book.

gilding powder. A fine powder, similar to powdered resin, used for sticking gold-leaf lettering or decorations to the covers.

glair. Albumen or white of egg beaten up with water, used in finishing, to stick gold leaf to cover material.

gluing up. Gluing over the back of a book to hold the sections together and in place.

gouge. A tool used for inscribing or tooling curved lines or arcs on book covers and backs.

grooves. The shoulders made when backing a book.

half-bound. A book having cloth or paper sides, with back and corners of leather or some other material.

handle letters. Brass letters with attached handles sometimes used for stamping.

head. The top of a book.

headcap. A fold of leather turned over to cover the headbands in some fine bindings.

hinge. The back of sections.

jog up. To even up the back, head, or tail of a book or stack of sections by holding loosely and tapping them on the top of the bench.

joints. The hinge between the boards and the back of a book.

kettle stitch. The catch stitch or knot made near the head and tail after sewing each section.

knocking-down iron. An iron plate placed under sections when knocking out the bend at the hinge.

lacing in. The threading or lacing in of the ends of cords (slips) through holes in the boards.

lettering pallet. A hand type holder for stamping books.

lining. Making or putting the lining in the back of a book.

lying press. A wooden screw press used for backing and sometimes for stamping. It has guides on the opposite side for the plow, and when inverted is the cutting press.

marbling. Coloring end papers or book edges by flowing colors on the surface of a size solution.

marking up. Drawing lines across the back of a book to show the position of saw cuts, tapes, or cords.

millboard. A stiff black cardboard used for book boards.

miter. A pallet with the lines cut off on a slant for tooling corners.

morocco. A leather made from goatskins much used in binding.

octavo. A section made of a sheet folded into eight leaves.

overcasting. A method of holding together single sheets or of strengthening a section or sections by sewing over the back.

page. One side of a leaf.

pallet. A tool for inscribing a line or design across the back of a book in blind or gold tooling.

paste papers. Quarter sheets of newspapers or other paper used under sheets being pasted.

pasting up. Pasting together the back edges of the first and last few sections. Prevents slipping when gluing up.

plow (or plough). A device used for cutting or trimming books. It consists of two parts joined by a hand screw, one part sliding in guides on the cutting press, and the other carrying the cutting blade.

pulling. Taking apart magazines or a book to be bound.

quarto. A section made up of four leaves or eight pages.

quire. Twenty-four sheets.

ream. Originally 20 quires or 480 sheets. The printer buys paper by the ream of 500 sheets.

register. To line up or match the printing on the leaves of a sheet. Such sheets are so printed and folded that the printing occupies exactly the same position on each page.

roll. A brass disk with lines or decorative pattern on the edge, used for decorating books.

sawing in. Sawing the back for sewing.

section. Usually one sheet when folded, but occasionally more than one sheet, sometimes called a "signature."

sextodecimo. A section of 16 leaves or 32 pages.

signature. The identifying letter or figure placed at the foot of the first page of each sheet or section. A term sometimes used for a section.

slips. The ends of the tapes or the frayed-out ends of the cords.

square. The part of the board that projects beyond the edges of the book.

tail. The foot or bottom edge of a book.

tape. Linen or cotton braid upon which books are sewed.

trimming. Cutting only the edges of the larger or projecting sheets. Sometimes done to show that a book has not been cut too deeply.

tub. A frame used to support the cutting or lying press.

type holder. A hand holder for a line of type when stamping.

uncut. A book is uncut when its edges have not been cut or are only lightly trimmed.

vellum. A parchment of calfskin used for bookbinding or as a writing material.

Bibliography

A.L.A., "Library Binding Manual," 1951, paper, $1.50, American Library Association, 50 E. Huron St., Chicago 11, Ill.

Banister, M., "Pictorial Manual of Bookbinding," 1958, $3.75, Ronald Press Co., 15 E. 26th St., New York 10, N. Y.

Cockerell, Douglas, "Bookbinding and the Care of Books," 1954, $4.95, Pitman Publishing Co., 2 W. 45th St., New York 36, N. Y.

Collins, Arthur F., "Book Crafts for Juniors," 1948, $3.50, Charles A. Bennett Co., 237 N. Monroe St., Peoria 3, Ill.
—— "Book Crafts for Seniors," 1938, $3.75, Bennett.

Diehl, Edith, "Bookbinding, Its Background and Technique," 1946, 2 vols., $30, Rinehart & Co., 232 Madison Ave., New York 16, N. Y.

Groneman, Chris, "General Bookbinding," 1958, paper, $1.50, Taplinger Publishing Co., 119 W. 57th St., New York 19, N. Y.

Hewitt-Bates, J. S., "Bookbinding," rev. ed., 1954, $3, Bennett.

Kitson, Edward, "Bookbinding," paper, 75 cents, Dover Publications, 920 Broadway, New York 10, N. Y.

Lewis, Arthur W., "Basic Bookbinding," 1955, paper, $1.35, Dover.

Smith, Frederick R., "Bookbinding," 1944, $2.25, Pitman.

Town, Laurence, "Bookbinding by Hand," 1952, $5, Pitman.

Dealers in Bookbinding Supplies

Demco Library Supplies, Madison 1, Wis., and New Haven 2, Conn.

Gane Brothers and Lane, Inc., 1335 W. Lake St., Chicago 7, Ill.; 4115 Forest Park Blvd., St. Louis, Mo.; 184 Second St., San Francisco, Calif.; 140 W. 17th St., Los Angeles 15, Calif.

Gane Bros. & Co. of New York Inc., 480 Canal St., New York 13, N. Y.

Gaylord Brothers, Inc., Syracuse, N. Y., and Stockton, Calif.

Index

Oakland Public Schools
Book Due

13-0620-05 180M1159-5